THE GRACES (E.M., W.G. & G.F.)

THE GRACES

(E.M., W.G. & G.F.)

by

A. G. POWELL

and

S. CANYNGE CAPLE

CEDRIC CHIVERS
PORTWAY
BATH

First Published 1948
by
The Cricket Book Society
This edition published
by
Cedric Chivers Ltd
Portway, Bath
as a
New Portway Special Reprint
by arrangement with the copyright holder
at the request of
The London & Home Counties Branch
of
The Library Association
1974

ISBN 0 85997 075 2

Printed in Great Britain by
Redwood Press Ltd, Trowbridge, Wiltshire
Bound by Cedric Chivers Ltd, Bath

FOREWORD TO 1974 EDITION

I think I was some eight years old when the most famous name in cricket first impinged on my consciousness. That would make the date about 1915, the year in which the Champion died, and it may have been his death that led to the conversation in question. A visitor to our house was chatting with my father in my presence and, the talk turning to cricket, remarked that he had once "seen Grace play". Seeing that I was puzzled, my father explained that Grace was "the greatest cricketer who ever lived".

This only increased my bewilderment. I had, I fancy, already handled a bat in the back garden, and I knew enough about cricket to regard it as a game for boys. It surprised me that the greatest of all players should have been a girl called Grace.

In the years that followed, however, I learned much more about Dr. W. G. Grace and his brothers, and I have, I suppose, read a pretty good proportion of the many books devoted to this astonishing family. Among them all I have enjoyed few more than this one, which first appeared in a limited edition to celebrate the centenary of 'W. G.'s' birth and is now re-published after more than a quarter of a century.

The culmination of my years of study of the Graces came when I attended, in 1971, the match to celebrate the centenary of the Thornbury Club, associated for all time with the memory of Dr. E. M. Grace. There were at least two 'E. M'.s' on the ground that day, for it is a tradition among the Little Doctor's descendants that the famous initials are repeated in each generation. Two descendants of the original 'E. M.' were playing in the match, on opposite sides. But what impressed me most was the enclosure roped off for members of the Grace family, an imposing and indeed formidable array, most courteous to anybody introduced to them but very much a clan of their own, admitting no outsider to their Holy of Holies.

It was on that day that I met Mr. S. Canynge Caple, joint author of this book. Mr. Caple, well known as an authority on the Graces, has brought all his literary skill to his collaboration with the late A. G. Powell, who died some years ago as a nonagenarian and who knew 'E. M.' and 'W. G.' personally. The result is a peculiarly vivid narrative, bringing the glorious brotherhood before our eyes as few authors have succeeded in doing.

What a wonderful collection they were, these brethren who between them dominated the world of cricket for half a century! To me 'E. M.' has always seemed the greatest – not as a cricketer of course, but as a character. 'E. M.' who once declared his side's innings closed while the ball was in the air so that he could claim his first declaration ever; 'E. M.' who was hit for 32 sixes by W. Hyman but refused to take himself off, 'E. M.' against whom no umpire within 20 miles of Thornbury dared give a leg-before-wicket decision.

'W. G.' however, is of course the central figure, as he must be of any book on the Graces. Never has any man imposed his personality on a game with such majesty or for so long as he. In a class-dominated age this son of a West Country doctor had dukes and princes bowing to his will.

But all the brothers were forceful characters, except perhaps the mild-mannered 'G. F.' who was only *29* when he died. The two eldest made little impact on cricket but they were true Graces in their lives, and rightly have their place in the pages that follow.

Anybody who wants to know what the Graces were really like should read their exploits as related by Powell and Caple.

Patrick Morrah.
June 1974

PUBLISHER'S NOTE

Although this book has been written by A. G. Powell and
S. Canynge Caple in collaboration the personal references
under the word " I " refer to A. G. Powell, whose contact
with the Gloucestershire C.C.C. covers the majority of the
period to which this book refers.

Edward Mills Grace

W. G. Grace
1906

G. F. Grace

Foreword.

I feel very honoured to have been asked to write a short Foreword for this book which is being published in the year of the centenary of W. G.

Being one of the younger members of the family, I was only able to watch my Father E.M. and Uncle W.G. play when they were well past their prime, but what impressed me most was my Father's marvellous fielding daringly close in at Point, the amazing quickness of eye and hand, also his cunningly flighted and very accurate lob-bowling. W. G. seemed to possess an uncanny gift of being able to place the ball when batting anywhere between the fielders, and very few balls were allowed to pass his bat. Also when bowling, his slow round-arm with his short, shuffling run, he would often change the position of his deep square leg fieldsman a few yards and the batsman would hit his next ball straight into his hands.

The three Brothers played every game for the game's sake, win or lose, with all their might and throughly enjoyed the fun, so great were their powers of observation, quick-thinking and skill.

In " The Graces, E.M., W.G. & G.F." Messrs. A. G. Powell and S. Canynge Caple have given a very faithful account of the family's deeds which I can strongly recommend to all readers and lovers of cricket.

EDGAR M. GRACE.

July, 1948

CHAPTER 1

It is not our intention in this volume to deal solely with the career of Dr. W. G. Grace, but to take the Grace Family as a whole and, where possible, to throw fresh light upon their wonderful achievements, not only on the cricket field, where they excelled, but in every phase of sport into which they entered.

Dr. Henry Mills Grace, the father of the five brothers Grace, was a Somerset man, being born at Long Ashton which is just outside the boundary of the City and County of Bristol. Described by his son ("W.G.") in his reminiscences as "a fair cricketer," there can be no doubt as to his great enthusiasm for the game for, when a medical student and unable to find any other time to practise, he would get up at four in the morning and go up on to Durdham Downs, Clifton, with his friends, where they would indulge in cricket from 5 a.m. to 8 a.m.

In 1831, Dr. Grace married a Miss Martha Pocock and settled down with a practice at Downend in Gloucestershire, some four miles out of Bristol. Less than two years later, on January 31st, 1833, the first of his sons, Henry, was born; and from the time he first went to school in 1841, could talk of nothing but cricket. It was not, however, until 1840 that the second son, Alfred, was born, while the following year (1841) saw the arrival of Edward Mills (E.M.), who was afterwards to be known as "The Coroner." After a lapse of seven years came "The Champion"—William Gilbert (W.G.), who first saw light on July 18th, 1848—a particularly eventful day in the annals of English cricket—and two years later was born the last of the brotherhood, the brilliant but ill-fated Fred (G.F.).

Although by nature of his calling an extremely busy man, Dr. Grace was one of the leading sportsmen in the Downend district and, when he could find the time, indulged in a little club cricket. So keen was he on the game that he had a cricket pitch laid down in the garden at Downend House and by insisting that his sons should practise regularly, he sowed in them those seeds which were to yield such a fine harvest in after years.

Apart from his love of cricket, Dr. Grace was a great hunting enthusiast and, being a personal friend of the Duke of Beaufort, often enjoyed a day with the hounds at Badminton; he kept this up regularly every winter until his death at the age of sixty-three. A most temperate man, he never smoked and, where drink was concerned, his quantum was a glass of wine with his dinner and an occasional whisky and water before retiring for the night.

It was thanks to the initiative of Dr. H. M. Grace that the Mangotsfield Cricket Club was formed—the team being composed of players from the neighbouring villages, while the matches were played on Rodway Hill Common. It speaks much for the enthusiasm of the Club members that Rodway Hill Common, which was a very rough piece of land and had to be levelled, was made suitable for cricket entirely at the expense of the Club; yet it was done. Eventually the Mangotsfield Cricket Club amalgamated with the Coalpit Heath Club, the combined clubs being known as " The West Gloucestershire Cricket Club." The result of this amalgamation served to make Dr. Grace keener than ever and he prevailed upon several good friends living in Bristol to join him in this newly formed venture. Foremost among those who responded to his call was Mrs. Grace's brother, Alfred Pocock, who twice a week walked twelve miles from Bristol to Rodway Hill Common and back to take part in the practice games.

Dr. H. M. Grace, who stood about 5 ft. 10 ins. high and weighed close on 13 stone, batted right-handed but, in both bowling and fielding, used his left hand. As captain of the team, he took his duties—especially that of picking a team— very seriously, always insisting on first of all choosing " two good bowlers, two good change bowlers, a wicket-keeper and a long stop. The rest, providing they can bat and field well, will make up a fair team." A good fielder himself, he made it a point that his team should be well up to standard in this important branch of the game and insisted on throwing and catching practice all round the field. Another excellent rule of his was that on at least one evening every week sides should be chosen and a practice match played with all the seriousness of a proper game.

With two such excellent cricketers as Dr. Grace and Alfred Pocock in the XI, the West Gloucestershire Club proved more than a match for most of the other local teams, the strongest of which was Lansdown formed as early as 1825. In 1845, the year before the amalgamation with Coalpit Heath, two nephews of Mrs. Grace (William Rees and George Gilbert) joined the Mangotsfield Club and proving themselves a great acquisition to the Club, continued to play regularly until their departure from Downend in 1852.

It was in 1848 that Henry, the eldest of the family, made his debut for West Gloucestershire at the early age of fifteen and, by a strange coincidence, " W.G." was born in that year. Although not very successful at first, Henry practised hard and in 1851 was able to return a batting average of 17, while also proving himself to be a very useful bowler.

The loss of his two nephews, Rees and Gilbert, who had to give up cricket in favour of serious work in 1852, left Dr. Grace with the task of finding suitable substitutes for them in the team   Fortunately Alfred (" Uncle ") Pocock was still available, while young Henry, now nineteen years of age, was improving steadily season by season; in fact, uncle and nephew were generally considered the best all-rounders in the district.

It was in the September and October of this year that two rather remarkable matches between Thornbury and Bristol took place and, in the first engagement in which both Henry and " Uncle " Pocock took part for the latter team, Thornbury were badly beaten.   Despite the failure on the part of his team, Mr. Williams, the Thornbury captain, offered to play Bristol again the following month for £25 a side, a challenge which Bristol very naturally accepted.   When Dr. Grace heard of it, he was most annoyed at the prospect of gambling being introduced into cricket, and more especially as Thornbury did not stand a chance.   He, therefore, offered to play for Thornbury, a very welcome offer in view of the fact that the Bristol team was stronger than before.   Before the game could be started, however, a most unfortunate situation arose for, when on the request of the Bristol captain the stake money was posted, the latter had to admit that he had not brought his part and, in the face of extreme indignation on the part of Dr. Grace and Mr. Williams, he had to prevail upon the members of his team, who were in a similar predicament, to hand over their watches and what little money they had in lieu of the stake.

Thornbury won the toss and on the advice of Dr. Grace, batted first. The Doctor and Mr. Williams opened the innings to the bowling of young Henry and " Uncle " Pocock and, by steady batting, they had scored 60 in 90 minutes before Mr. Williams was bowled for a really brilliant 45. Dr. Grace was then not out 12; half-an-hour later the innings closed for 75, the Doctor carrying his bat for a stubborn 17. As the match had started rather later than had been expected, Bristol did not begin to bat until half past three but, as with the exception of Dr. Grace there was no bowler of any note on the Thornbury side, it was thought that the match would be over in Bristol's favour by five o'clock. It was, however, over earlier than that. Snow having fallen during the day, the wicket cut up badly and, with the Doctor bowling as steadily as he had batted and Mr. Williams getting a wicket nearly every over with fast underhand " sneaks," Bristol were put out for under 50 runs by 4.45 p.m. Of course the Bristol team were laughed at generally for their failure while, on their return to Downend, Henry and " Uncle " Pocock had to endure much banter and chaff from the family and their sporting friends; in fact, it was some time before they were allowed to forget the second match with Thornbury.

In 1850, with the family still increasing at regular intervals, the accommodation at Downend House was found to be inadequate and a move was made to " The Chestnuts," where Dr. and Mrs. Grace were to spend the remainder of their lives. It should be stated here that Mrs. Grace took a great interest in the game and was every bit as enthusiastic over it as were her husband, brother and sons. She would drive to all the important matches in her pony cart from which she watched every ball that was bowled.

Mrs. Grace's father, Mr. George Pocock, was the proprietor of the most popular private boarding school in the city of Bristol, in addition to which he was by way of being something of a local character for early in the XIXth Century he created quite a sensation by travelling all over the country in a kite carriage. At Ascot Races in June, 1828, he came under the notice of no less a personage than King George IV. Another of Pocock's numerous inventions was a machine for inflicting punishment on his scholars; this, however, was not quite so popular.

There is no doubt that certain members of the Grace family —notably " E.M." and " W.G."—inherited from " Grand-father " Pocock traits of character which are familiar to all who knew them. George Pocock was the organist of Portland Wesleyan Church at Kingsdown, near Bristol, and in addition to playing the instrument, owned it. Unfortunately for the church, there arose a sad disagreement between the organist and the deacons, each side wanting their own way over certain matters, and at last Mr. Pocock, being unable either to force his point or obtain a compromise, not only refused to play any more but, leaving the church, took with him the organ upon which he contributed so important a part of the Sabbath services.

A similar incident in which his grandson " E.M." figured in his youth is recalled by that wonderful nonagenerian sports-man, the late Mr. W. Hayes Olive, who tells us that when he and " E.M." were at school together at Kempe's School, Long Ashton, history repeated itself. This time, however, it was the wickets not the organ that were removed. It appears that the boys were playing cricket and " E.M.," who was batting, received a crack on the leg from a shooter. " How's that? " piped a small shrill voice. " OUT " came the chorus of other shrill voices; but " E.M." wouldn't go. They argued and argued as small boys will and eventually, being overborne by numbers, " E.M." had to go—BUT HE PULLED UP THE STUMPS AND TOOK THEM WITH HIM.

As a matter of cricket interest, it is worth noting that Kempe's School at Long Ashton probably produced as many good cricketers as any private establishment in or around Bristol. Two of Dr. Grace's sons were educated there— Alfred and Edward (E.M.)—as well as W. W. F. Pullen and Cuthbert Kempe, both of whom subsequently played for Gloucestershire. The school, which was founded early in the XIXth Century by a Mr. Husbands, was acquired by Mr. John Kempe in 1845, and he was succeeded as proprietor and master by his son, Wilfred Kempe.

Returning to the Pococks, from whom the Graces descended on their mother's side, we find that they were really a most remarkable family.   One of them in the XVIIIth Century was a notable artist of marine subjects: a fine example of his work can be seen in the Merchants' Hall, Bristol, while several others are exhibited at the Bristol Art Gallery.   To Alfred (" Uncle ") Pocock, brother of Mrs. Grace, who has already been mentioned, belongs perhaps more than to anyone else the credit of laying the foundations of that wonderful cricket skill, which all the Grace boys developed very early in life and which was to bring immortal fame to three of them.   In addition to the five boys, there were four daughters to whom has been attributed wonderful prowess as cricketers.   This, however, is not in accordance with actual fact for, although there can be little doubt that they were on occasions " roped in " to bowl and field while the boys practised batting, I think this was the extent of their cricket careers.

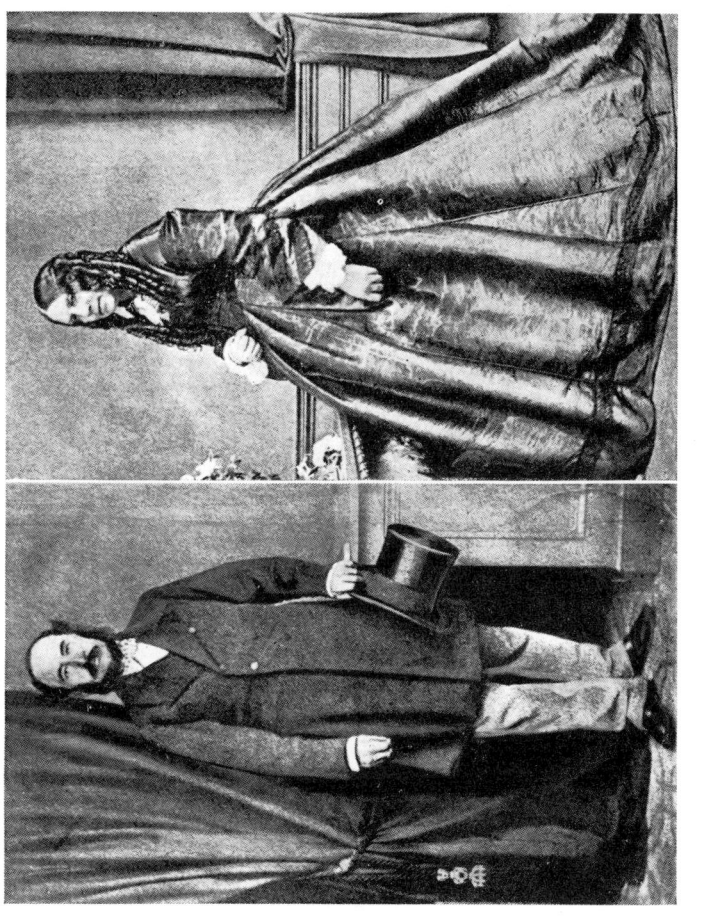

DR. GRACE, SEN.   MRS. GRACE

THE PARENTS OF E.M., W.G. & G.F.

CHAPTER II

1854 was a Red Letter Year in the lives of the Grace family, for in June of that year the West Gloucestershire Club met for the first time an All-England XI, captained by William Clarke, in the fields at the back of the Full Moon Hotel, near Stokes Croft, Bristol. Such an historic match as this must be related in full detail and here is a report of the game which appeared in " The Bristol Mercury and Felix Farley's Journal " (this incidentally was the first cricket report to be published in Bristol).

Although Dr. W. G. Grace in one of his several volumes of reminiscences states that this match was organised by his father, the old newspaper report gives the credit for arranging the game to Mr. Wintle, landlord of " The Full Moon Hotel."

" The All-England men," says the report, " were paid £65 for their services by Mr. Wintle, by whom they were brought down to engage a double number of amateurs, Mr. Wintle hoping to make it a good speculation.

The account then goes on to state that " the All-England men travelled all night after having finished a match in Leicestershire, to be in Bristol by Thursday. It is said that they make £200 each during the year by their play."

In his reminiscences, " W.G." said he remembered driving to see the ground, which was being prepared by his father's gardener and other men; " the field " was originally a ridge and furrow field and had been specially re-laid the previous autumn. The pitch was first rate but the outfield and other parts of the ground were very rough and uneven. " The Champion " goes on to say that he watched the match in company with his mother, who sat in her pony cart and saw every ball bowled. The main thing that struck little Gilbert (he was only six years old) was that several members of the All-England XI wore tall hats.

Continuing with the contemporary account published in the
" Bristol Times," we read that " it is easy to realise what an
interesting scene it must have been. The tents in the field were
conveniently pitched and, at twelve o'clock noon on Thursday,
the wickets were also pitched for the first time; there being a
printing press on the ground to chronicle the performances at
the close of each day's play. At first the field did not fill
rapidly with a strong company but the practised eye soon
discovered 'that those who attended were keen lovers and
ardent amateurs of the game. Towards three o'clock, however,
a larger concourse assembled, while numbers of jolly citizens
sat under tents—Turk-like—enjoying their pipes of peace and
tankards of home brewed."

" We are but scantily versed in this fine exercise," confesses
the writer of this first cricket report to appear in a Bristol
paper, " but we believe all the etiquette usual between con-
tending parties was observed in this case, but from whom the
peaceable cartel emanated we cannot say. Of this, however,
we are satisfied that both behaved courteously as they are
doing their devoirs right manfully."

Concerning the actual progress of the game, the reporter of
over four score years ago has little to say. " Being scantily
versed in the manly exercise," he very wisely confines himself
to bare details. " Having won the toss," he states, " the All-
England XI went in first and scored 108; the first six batsmen
scored between 80 and 90, and the others went out rather
quickly . . . twelve of the West Gloucestershire men got 33
by seven o'clock when the wickets were struck for the day.
It was pretty clear that the county gentlemen, however fair
their play, had little chance against eleven picked men, as at
one time only two runs were scored in 35 minutes." " Things
most admired of the day," says the report, " were the catching
of Messrs. Caffyn and Sydney—who goes by the classical name
of ' Julius Cæsar.' We may mention also that only one
casualty occurred to one of the Gloucestershire batsmen, who
had his thumb dislocated by a ball."

In a shorter report on the second day's play, the reporter
states that " the last lift their score got was from the batting
of Mr. Jones, who told four with one swipe but went down
in his turn before the artful bowling of George Parr, the All-
England bowler."

The result of this now historic encounter was a crushing defeat for West Gloucestershire by 149 runs. Of the part played in the game by the Grace family, we find that Alfred Pocock, who opened the innings, scored 3 in the first innings and 18 at his second attempt, while in the field he distinguished himself by catching out two of his opponents. " Young " Henry, who went in first wicket down, had the misfortune to be caught by Caffyn off Clarke before he had scored in the first innings but, on batting a second time, more than redeemed this failure by making 15 before George Parr bowled him— incidentally Henry was one of the only four bats on the local side to reach double figures—while, as a bowler, he secured 3 wickets. The last member of the family, Dr. Grace, was dismissed for 0 and 3 but made one catch.

I append here the actual score sheet of the match, which has only once been reproduced since the year 1854.

ALL ENGLAND.

A. CLARK, c Strachan, b Ray	2	c Pocock, b Jones	11
BICKLEY, c Pocock, b H. Grace	23	c Grace, b Coddington	6
S. PARR, c Smallbones, b Marchant	19	c and b Marchant	7
W. CAFFYN, lbw, b Marchant	2	b Jones	39
G. PARR, st Kingston, b Marchant	20	c and b Marchant	43
J. CAESAR, st Kingston, b Marchant	21	c Simpson, b Pocock	10
G. ANDERSON, not out	14	b Grace	6
F. BOX, c Capel, b Marchant	0	c Capel, b Coddington	23
J. A. MARSHALL, b Marchant	1	b Jones	17
WILLSHER, b Marchant	2	b Grace	0
W. CLARKE, b Marchant	0	not out	1
Leg-bye 1, wides 3	4	bye 1, wides 9	10
	108		**173**

WEST GLOUCESTERSHIRE XXII.

C. BRIGHT, c Caesar, b Bickley	1	b Bickley	3
A. POCOCK, c Caffyn, b Clarke	3	b Clarke	18
H. GRACE, c Caffyn, b Clarke	0	b G. Parr	15
J. PEPLER, b Bickley	0	b Caffyn	0
R. C. CAPEL, b Clarke	0	b Willsher	1
H. STRACHAN, b Clarke	0	b Caffyn	2
A. SMALLBONE, b Clarke	0	c Caffyn, b Bickley	0
J. SIMPSON, b Bickley	1	b Bickley	1
J. MILLER, c Willsher, b Clarke	0	b Clarke	2
C. BABER, c Caffyn, b Clarke	2	b Willsher	0
J. CODDINGTON, b Bickley	15	c Caffyn, b Clarke	0
J. PROTHEROE, c Bickley, b Clarke	0	b Caffyn	0
A. A. WILKIE, c Caesar, b Bickley	0	c Caffyn, b Clarke	0
P. O. KINGSTON, b Bickley	5	run out	0
E. TRINDER, run out	0	c Willsher, b Clarke	4
A. MARCHANT, run out	3	b Bickley	28
J. D. CAMPBELL, b Bickley	1	run out	0
C. J. B. MAIS, b Anderson	0	not out	0

R. W. TORRE, not out	1	c Anderson, b Clarke 0
Dr. H. M. GRACE, c Anderson, b Clarke	0	b Caffyn 3
C. F. QUINTON, c Bickley, b Clarke	2	c Willsher, b Bickley 0
A. M. JONES, b Bickley	5	b Clarke 0
Bye 1, leg-byes 3	4	byes 7, leg-byes 5 .. 12
	43	**89**

UMPIRES: Mynn (England), Oscroft (W. Gloucestershire).

It will be seen from this score sheet that the best member of the West Gloucestershire side was A. Marchant who, in addition to taking 10 wickets in the match, was also top scorer for his team with 28 in the second innings. For the All-England XI, Bickley's bowling analyses are worth quoting: —

1st Innings: 38 overs. 30 maidens. 10 runs. 8 wickets.

2nd Innings: 13 overs. 12 maidens. 2 runs. 5 wickets.

These figures give him the excellent record of 13 wickets for 12 runs.

William Clarke was even more successful in the number of wickets taken for he claimed 18 in the match, 11 in the first innings and 7 in the second. We are not told, however, how many runs were scored off him.

It is interesting to note in passing that the umpires for this famous match were Mynn for All-England and Oscroft for West Gloucestershire. Alfred Mynn, one of the most famous cricketers of all time, stood over six feet tall and weighed in his prime 20 stone; he was known both as " Alfred the Great " and " The Lion of Kent." He made his debut in 1832 under the patronage of Lord Sones (for cricketers in those days were adopted like prize fighters), and won his spurs by defeating Hills, who held the single wicket championship of England. Four years later, in a famous North v. South match at Leicester played for £500 a side, Mynn scored 21 not out and 125. For a period this veteran champion, who stood at one side of the wicket on the field behind the " Full Moon Hotel, Bristol," in June, 1854, dominated the game even as little William Gilbert Grace, sitting that day with his mother in her pony cart, was destined to do in after years.

The other umpire, Oscroft, was a great Nottinghamshire player in his day and uncle of the famous William Oscroft, who toured Australia with " W.G." in 1873.

Despite the trouncing they had received at the hands of the All-England XI, West Gloucestershire, nothing daunted, challenged their conquerors to a second game the following year on the same ground. In this match in which West Gloucestershire were even more heavily beaten than before (this time by no less than 165 runs), William Clarke did not take part but nevertheless was on the ground directing affairs.

A very notable point about this game was that it marked the debut of young " E.M." in representative cricket and although only fourteen years old, he appears to have distinguished himself in the field for at the end of the report in the " Bristol Mercury " appears this paragraph : —

> " We should mention that much attention was attracted during each innings of the XI to the extraordinary skill displayed by young Edward Grace at long-stop. So much admiration did it elicit that at the conclusion of the second innings William Clarke, who was on the ground, presented the youthful player with a bat as a reward."

It is worth noting that " E.M." had been especially fetched from school at Long Ashton to take part in the match. The score sheet shows that " E.M." went in at the end of a long procession and scored 1 in the first innings and 3 in the second. As there were no fewer than 20 " ducks " in the Club's two innings, this lad of thirteen years did not do so badly. In the first innings he was given out l.b.w. to Willsher. The ball hit him on the waistcoat, and he was very short as he did not grow to full height till he was 19. Was he satisfied with the decision, I wonder?

In suffering such a hollow defeat, the West Gloucestershire team could only total 48 and 78, of which Henry Grace (top scorer in the first innings) with 13, Dr. Grace (top scorer in the second innings) with 16, and " Uncle " Pocock with 15 were the only men to reach double figures. For All-England, Julius Cæsar scored 33 and 78.

> " It must have been very mortifying for the crack men of the 'provincial club," says the " Mercury," " to see their foremost players sent to the right about one after another. The fielding of the professionals was admirable; the celerity and certainty of their movements never allowing the throwing away of a chance while, on the other hand, it was impossible not to see that the West

Gloucestershire batting with few exceptions suffered from over-cautiousness not to allow themselves to be taken at a disadvantage. For the greater part there seemed to be too great a tendency to content themselves to watching for the well-directed balls that were aimed at their wickets and the bat was seldom raised to give a vigorous blow, while such was the fielding of the England XI that none but vigorous blows would allow of any running."

From this report we have conclusive proof that the demand for brighter cricket is no new thing and that then, as now, the game suffered from lack of vigorous blows.

The name of William Clarke, who captained the All-England XI in the match at Stokes Croft in 1854 and was present at the second game the following year, is probably unknown except to those who have studied the history of the game, but this famous Nottinghamshire player did a great service to the game of cricket by founding the All-England XI and taking them to many parts of the country for exhibition matches. Born in 1798, he was therefore 56 years of age when he brought his team to Bristol; think of it! Captain of an All-England team at 56 years of age! Nowadays a cricketer is a " veteran " at 40. He died in 1856.

There was in the All-England XI in 1855 a player, R. C. Tinley, who later achieved what no other first class cricketer ever did. He succeeded in dismissing Dr. W. G. Grace for a " duck " in each innings when the champion was playing for XXII of Bath against an All-England XI at Lansdowne in 1864. Tinley was a slow underhand bowler.

As Bristol has been much built over in recent years, the field in Stokes Croft, where these historic matches took place, no longer exists, and it seems a great pity that there is nothing to record the fact that these games were played there. The purpose could be well served by the erection of a tablet outside the " Full Moon Hotel," worded something like this: —

" NEAR THIS SPOT IN THE YEAR 1854 TOOK PLACE THE FIRST REPRESENTATIVE CRICKET MATCH IN GLOUCESTER-SHIRE BETWEEN WILLIAM CLARKE'S ALL-ENGLAND XI AND XXII OF WEST GLOUCESTERSHIRE CAPTAINED BY DR. HENRY MILLS GRACE, THE FATHER OF MESSRS. E. M., W. G. AND G. F. GRACE, OF IMMORTAL MEMORY."

CHAPTER III.

The boyhood of the Graces was typical of the country life of Mid-Victorian days; sport in variety filled their leisure hours and among the accomplishments acquired by young Gilbert—as " W.G." was known when a boy—before reaching his 'teens, was to shoot straight. Nowadays there is little game to be had at Downend but in those days the boys were able to get a shot at woodcock, rabbits and even hares without having to venture far from home. This phase of sport never ceased to appeal to " W.G." and later you will read of some of his exploits with the gun when out with his friend, the late Mr. Herbert Gibbs.

" W.G.'s " education began at a school in Downend village conducted by Miss Trotman, who little thought that this sturdy young member of her modest establishment was destined to become not only one of the greatest figures in the world of cricket but in English sporting life generally, or that the little village school over which she presided would have a permanent place in history on account of its associations with the childhood of " The Champion of Cricketers! "

A Mr. Curtis of Winterbourne next took a hand in young Gilbert's education and from here he passed on to Rudgway House School, the proprietor and master of which was Mr. Malpas. Nothing, however, of outstanding interest either at work or play is recorded during " W.G.'s " sojourn with Mr. Malpas and, leaving him at the age of fourteen, he received the advantage of private tuition from the Rev. J. W. Dann, who subsequently married one of his pupil's sisters. There must be many who still remember well that fine old sporting cleric, who was for many years a familiar figure at Gloucestershire matches, naturally taking great pride in the Grace's cricket achievements.

It must always be remembered that the Grace boys had advantages in their cricket training which few others have had, for not only were they intensively coached almost as soon as

they were big enough to hold a bat, but all of them were
introduced to good class cricket long before the average lad
could find the opportunity. " W.G." was only nine years old
when he was included in the West Gloucestershire side against
Bedminster. Has any other youngster of that age taken part
in a local game of such importance? I doubt it. Bedminster
then, as now, were one of the strongest teams in the Bristol
area and one would like to know what the fielders thought
when they saw this boy of nine coming out to bat. He succeeded, however, in scoring 3 not out. The score-book of
this match, which was played on July 19th, 1857, would make
interesting reading if it could be found. During that season
the future champion also appeared in two games against
Clifton, but only aggregated 1 run in 3 innings. The following year, playing for West Gloucestershire in home and
away matches against Bedminster and once against Clifton,
he totalled only 4 runs in 6 innings, while in 1859 he had
9 innings for but 12 runs. If at that time there was any
competition for places in the West Gloucestershire team, then
there must have been much grumbling at the carrying of so
juvenile a passenger. In 1860, however, the faith of Dr. Grace
in his young son, Gilbert, was fully justified for, chosen to
play against Clifton on July 19th and 20th, he went in eighth
(his brother " E.M." having already scored 150 and " Uncle "
Pocock 44), and was not out 35 at the drawing of stumps.
Next day he went on to make 51 and admitted afterwards
that not one of his greatest innings in first class matches gave
him more satisfaction than this, his first 50 made at the early
age of twelve. His record for the season was 82 runs in 4
innings but the following season brought him much disappointment as in 10 innings he could only collect 46 runs and,
although scoring 54 in five knocks in 1862, it was not until
1863 that he enjoyed his first consistent season. During that
season, aged 15, he began to play really seriously and in 19
innings totalled no less than 350 runs, not against boys like
himself but against the best gentlemen cricketers of the day,
many of them 'Varsity men and excellent players. In view
of this fact I make no apology for giving his figures for West
Gloucestershire in full: —

v. Clifton	86 and 5 not out.
v. Knowle Park	18 and 21 not out.
v. Lansdown	9 and 10 not out.

    v. Gentlemen of Devon 15 not out and 4.
    v. XXII of Corsham   3.
    v. Gentlemen of Devon 19 and 1.
    v. Somerset   52 not out and 1.
    v. Cheltenham College 25 and 2.

His average was 26.12.

A remarkable feature of his successes was that early in 1863 he became dangerously ill with pneumonia (at one time his life was despaired of) and, although unable to take part in any cricket at the commencement of the season, was able to turn out in July, a wonderful tribute to his fine constitution.

No opportunity for getting a game was ever lost by this remarkable cricketing family and by this time clubs had sprung up in most of the neighbouring villages. Enthusiasm for the game, inspired very largely by the great keenness of Dr. H. M. Grace, was evident all round; it must be remembered that this was an age of limited pleasures and even more limited means of getting about. Naturally there was tremendous rivalry between the country clubs, and one of these village battles between Hanham and Bitton produced a finish that was talked of for years afterwards. Two of the Graces, Henry and Gilbert (W.G.), had been invited to strengthen the Hanham team and, just as they were setting off in the pony-trap, " E.M." appeared, complete with cricketing gear. His brothers looked surprised and, on enquiring where he was going, were none too pleased to find that Edward, who had not been included in the invitation to play for Hanham, intended to go and take his chance. " It's no good," said " W.G." " The other side won't stand three of us." But " E.M.," not to be put off, got in the trap and went with his brothers. The game was to be played at Bitton and here, when the Graces arrived, the local stalwarts gave the irrepressible " E.M." a great welcome. At first Henry and " W.G." were puzzled until it dawned on them . . . brother Ted belonged to the enemy's camp!

The scene on this delightful summer's afternoon can be imagined by anyone who has had the experience of village cricket, which is considered by many to be the jolliest and keenest sort of cricket.

Bitton is a pleasant little place mid-way between Bath and Bristol on the Gloucestershire side of the Avon and, incidentally, has changed but little since the days of this famous battle with Hanham. On this auspicious occasion Hanham, with Henry and Gilbert Grace, both already famous in the eyes of these village enthusiasts, won the toss but, unfortunately for the visitors, the brothers Grace in company with the rest of the team failed to come off, much to the delight of the home supporters who, numbering more than half the population of Bitton, were scattered round the field. When the last Hanham wicket fell, the score was only 51. Then Bitton batted and, making better use of the wicket than their opponents had done, totalled 81. On Hanham going in for the second time, they fared even worse than before and, being put out for 39, the game seemed as good as over. The home team only requiring a mere 10 runs to win, some of the Hanham supporters left the ground in despair and disgust. " Call this cricket," said one outspoken critic. " Why I haven't seen a decent hit yet." " E.M.," hearing this remark, replied that he would soon put that right and went in to take the first over from his brother Henry. The pitch, however, was as usual in those days unreliable; one ball might fly off the ground head high, while the next would prove to be a shooter. The first ball Ted received from his brother was a shooter; moreover it shot from the spot upon which it pitched at an angle of 45 degrees—at least, that is what the batsman told the others in the dressing-room who were preparing to go home. Further explanations were interrupted by a cheer; someone had hit a three. Then there came a groan; someone was out. A fellow had to change back hastily into his flannels to fill the vacancy, and soon the others were busy undressing. Henry at one end and Gilbert at the other were making a clean sweep of the opposition and when the last man, who had been umpiring, came in four runs were still needed. " W.G.," however, diddled him by changing his action at the last moment; the batsman, who was expecting a fast overarm ball, being completely deceived by an underhand " daisy-cutter " which found its way on to the stumps. Thus the cream of Bitton cricket had been skimmed for 6 runs—three from the bat and three byes. I append the score-sheet of this very remarkable village cricket match, as I consider it a valuable contribution to cricket history.

HANHAM.

W. G. GRACE, c E. M. Grace, b Fraser ..	3	b E. M. Grace	10
T. HOWARD, run out	6	run out	1
J. WRIGHT, not out	16	c Fraser, b E. M. Grace	0
C. FRY, b Fraser	0	run out	1
J. RICHMOND, c Jones, b E. M. Grace ..	1	c Pillinger, b E. M. Grace ..	0
A. GRACE, c and b Fraser	2	b Pillinger	5
H. GRACE, b Fraser	7	b E. M. Grace	3
W. BUCKNALL, run out	1	b Pillinger	3
T. MORRIS, b E. M. Grace	0	st Pillinger, b E. M. Grace ..	8
A. BRYANT, run out	2	not out	1
B. SEALY, b E. M. Grace	10	lbw, b E. M. Grace	1
Extras	3	Extras	6
	51		**39**

BITTON.

E. M. GRACE, b H. Grace	7	b H. Grace	0
J. LILLINGTON, run out	2	b W. G. Grace	0
R. POLLINGER, b H. Grace	10	b H. Grace	0
F. JONES, b Howard	33	b W. G. Grace	0
C. FRASER, b W. G. Grace	2	run out	0
D. BUSH, b W. G. Grace	3	run out	3
A. WESTON, b W. G. Grace	3	c and b W. G. Grace	0
A. SOMERVILLE, run out	7	b W. G. Grace	0
H. BUSH, b W. G. Grace	0	not out	0
F. COX, b W. G. Grace	2	b W. G. Grace	0
J. GODFREY, b W. G. Grace	3	b W. G. Grace	0
Byes	9	Byes	3
	81		**6**

Result: Hanham won by 3 runs.

It will be noticed that the name A. Grace, presumably Alfred, appears in the Hanham team, thus no fewer than four of the Grace family took part in this famous match, while it is also interesting to note that of the 40 wickets that fell, W.G. took 12, E.M. 9 and Henry 4, making a total of 25. Another point of interest is that R. Pillinger, the Bitton wicket-keeper, was put on to bowl in Hanham's second innings and took two wickets.

CHAPTER IV

Considering that the Grace boys had to prepare like any
other lads for the real and serious battle of Life (they all went
into the medical profession), it is surprising to find them playing so much cricket. In the season of 1857, when " E.M."
was only 15 years old, he was constantly helping one side or
another; in fact, old newspaper files show that Bedminster,
Frenchay, Flax Bourton, Long Ashton, Clifton and West
Gloucestershire and other clubs as well numbered him among
their players. The reason why he was in such demand is easy
to find for he was a good bowler of fast round-arm stuff, a
batsman who defied the conventions and believed in the
" vigorous blow " theory no matter where the ball went, besides
being an excellent fielder who seldom, if ever, dropped a catch.
In one game against Redland he took nearly all the wickets
and that season Redland were one of the strongest clubs in
the district. In fact, they easily beat the strong Bedminster
side, " E.M." being out twice for 4 runs.

1862 saw " E.M." achieve great things in big cricket and
in the averages for the year, which included all games even
those against odds, he stood third to Robert Carpenter, grand-
father of the Essex batsman Jack O'Connor, and A. H. Faber.
It was in his first appearance in " The Canterbury Week " that
he created such a great sensation. Dr. and Mrs. Grace always
stayed with friends near Canterbury during the Week and,
while they were staying there in 1862, the Kent secretary,
finding they were a man short, approached the Doctor and
asked him to let " E.M." play. " E.M." happened to be at
home at Downend at the time and his father pointed out that
it was hardly worth while bringing the lad all the way from
Gloucestershire to play in one match; he would, however, send
for him if they would allow him to play for the M.C.C. against
Kent (the second match of the Week). The secretary agreed
and " E.M." was wired for. Arriving on the second day,
just in time for his innings, he was unfortunately dismissed
first ball. At his second attempt, however, he retrieved this

failure by scoring 56, an innings which was described as a very fine performance. This match was over at 3.30 p.m. and in those days three matches were played one after the other, as soon as one finished the next was begun. Unhappily before the M.C.C. match could be commenced a slight but unpleasant dispute arose, certain of the Kent players objecting to " E.M." representing the M.C.C. on the grounds that he was not a member of the club. It happened that the Kent secretary was not at hand when the dispute started but, on his return to the ground, he explained that he had given "E.M.'.' permission to play for the visitors and, this being settled, the match was begun. What a triumph for the young West Country player! After carrying his bat through the M.C.C. innings for 192 not out, he took all ten wickets in Kent's second innings. No doubt the Kent players wished they had been firm and not allowed him to play but there can be no gain-saying that his wonderful play delighted not a few of his opponents. Both his batting and bowling feats were rewarded, the President of the M.C.C., the Earl of Sefton, presenting him with a bat, while the Hon. Spencer Ponsonby had the ball with which he had taken all the Kent wickets mounted on an ebony stand, with the following inscription on a silver plate :—

WITH THIS BALL
(PRESENTED BY M.C.C. TO E. M. GRACE)
HE GOT EVERY WICKET IN 2ND INNINGS, IN THE
MATCH PLAYED AT CANTERBURY,
AUGUST 14TH & 15TH, 1862,
GENTLEMEN OF KENT V. M.C.C.
FOR WHOM HE PLAYED AS AN EMERGENCY, AND
IN WHICH, GOING IN FIRST,
HE SCORED
192 NOT OUT.

Another three-figure innings of his, 118 for South Wales against the M.C.C. at Lord's the same year, definitely estab-lished " E.M.'s " reputation as a first-class cricketer. In fact ne was as well known on cricket grounds throughout England as his brother Gilbert (who was seven years his junior) was to be some thirty years later.

In 1863 a match between a West Gloucestershire team and an All-England XI on Durdham Downs, Clifton, marked another milestone in the progress of representative cricket in Gloucestershire, only this time the title of the local XXII was altered to " Bristol and District." The All-England team, which was brought by George Parr, was probably the strongest combination of professional players that had yet appeared. Two teams had been touring the country for some time, one under the title of " All-England," while the other was known as " United All-England." Naturally great rivalry existed between them but, having combined their resources in order to tour Australia, this match with Bristol took place just prior to their departure for the Antipodes. The game was organised by a committee, who issued an appeal in the local papers, stating that they had been under considerable expense and hoping that subscriptions would be forthcoming " from those wishing to see the same properly applied."

The conditions under which cricket is now played have changed considerably since a few sportsmen made themselves responsible for the visit to Bristol of this famous All-England team; in one respect, however, cricket nowadays is the same as 85 years ago—expenses have to be incurred and money has to be found to pay the bills. The moving spirit in this visit of the All-England team to Bristol was a Mr. Sykes Bramhall, who took part in the match under the nom-de-plume of " Captain Rose." It would be interesting to learn more of this gentleman, who must have been a leading light in Bristol sporting circles and who figured in Police Court proceedings as the result of an incident arising out of the game.

Bristol itself seems to have been deeply stirred by this very attractive sporting event and, side by side with the latest despatches concerning the war between the Northern and Southern States of America, there appeared in a Bristol newspaper the following paragraph: —

" This day week will be commenced a great match on Durdham Downs, between All-England and XXII of Bristol and neighbourhood, and a treat will unquestionably be enjoyed by all who attend for not only will the game itself be exhibited almost to perfection but the marvellous agility and vigour displayed will equal, if not surpass, what we read of in the games of Ancient Greece and Rome and in the tournaments of the Middle Ages.

" The Eleven, in all probability, will consist of the following:—Parr, Jackson, H. H. Stephenson, Tinley, Willsher, A. Clark, G. Anderson, Carpenter, Hayward, Tarrant and Rowbotham. It would be difficult to get a much stronger selection than this including, as it does, members of the All-England and United teams, and if our local amateurs achieve a victory over them it will be something to be proud of. Every part of the game will be efficiently sustained and the committee were justified in asserting that they feel assured this match will greatly tend to promote and improve cricket in the neighbourhood."

That the committee fully realised the value of advance publicity is certain for odds and ends appeared almost daily in the only local daily paper of that period—" The Western Daily Press." The selection of the XXII, however, caused a deal of anxiety, various hints as to the lucky ones appearing in paragraphs commencing " We hear . . . " before the official list under big type headings appeared as follows:—

" Captain Rose," the Rev. J. Mirehouse, Henry Grace, Alfred Grace, E. M. Grace, W. G. Grace, D. Bernard, J. Sewell, E. Howsin, T. H. Hill, W. Jones, T. E. Danbery, W. E. Mirehouse, J. F. Fussell, A. Dane, J. D. P. Trenfield, G. Gibbs, J. Pillinger J. D. Donoghue and R. Brotherhood.

Two vacancies were left to be filled later; unfortunately the names of the clubs to which the players belonged are not given but in the list are some very interesting personalities. The four brothers Grace need neither introduction nor comment; Mr. J. Sewell was the father of C. O. H. Sewell, who afterwards captained the Gloucestershire county team for some time. D. Bernard was probably the sporting Bristol doctor who is remembered as a very good billiards player, while the brothers Mirehouse were members of a very prominent family of Bristol merchants. G. Gibbs was surely a member of the famous firm of gun manufacturers, while Pillinger was drawn from the Bedminster Club and was, as an old man, well known in the Knowle district. Lastly,

Brotherhood was probably a brother of Charles Brotherhood, who for many years played for the Bristol Bohemians.

At last the day of the match arrived, August 31st, 1863— the great occasion upon which William Gilbert Grace was to receive his baptism in important cricket; he was no more than 15 years old, and must have appeared extremely young to play in such distinguished company. A contemporary of his, now a very old man, has tried to conjure up a picture of what " W.G." was like at this time. " I recall him," he says, " as a lanky, loose-limbed youth with fuzzy hair already beginning to show on the sides of his face; for boys did not shave as they do now before they had done with the perambulator. In fact, ' W.G.' never stropped a razor in his life; he had the rugged physiognomy characteristics of the Graces, which made them all look more like farmers than doctors, and he was full of life and vim."

What an event this must have been in his young life and how anxious he must have been to justify his inclusion in this notable company of cricketers !

The scene must have been memorably interesting and it is much to be regretted that no pictorial record, as far as can be ascertained, was made. The reporter of the " Western Daily Press," however, helps us by his descriptive account to visualise the aspect of this part of the Downs on that famous day in August, 1863. A line of tents, the reporter states, provided accommodation for the privileged guests, in one of which Mr. Bale dispensed refreshments and served " a first-class ordinary each day at two o'clock." There were no tram cars nor motor cars then; one can imagine that both cricketers and spectators came to the ground in all sorts of vehicles, which would be parked along the edge of the Downs, as one would see them at coursing meetings in Wiltshire and up Cirencester way. The old-fashioned family coach would be there with a merry party from the country, women in crinolines and poke-bonnets, men in top hats and side-whiskers accompanying them, and endeavouring to explain to them the intricacies of the game. Without doubt, of course, Mrs. Grace was there in her pony carriage, feeling extremely proud that four of her five sons were playing. Her husband, the Doctor, being a very active member of the organising committee, would be busy seeing that all was in order for the start. It is

Dr. E. M. Grace

to be noted that Mr. J. W. Arrowsmith, for many years the official printer to the Gloucestershire Club, had a printing press on the ground and provided the public with score cards at the fall of each wicket.

At length all was ready for the game to commence and George Parr, who apparently captained the visitors from the pavilion for his name does not appear on the score-sheet, created quite a stir by winning the toss and putting his opponents in to bat. " No doubt," the newspaper account states, " he desired to give the locals a chance. H. H. Stephenson took the post of wicket-keeper, while E. M. Grace and D. Bernard opened the batting to the bowling of Tarrant and Willsher." The fall of a wicket was not long delayed for Bernard was out for a " duck," and then Jones came in. " The Eleven," it was reported, " seems hardly to have got into play for Jones was missed by Willsher at point and again by Julius Cæsar in the slips, off successive balls from Tarrant." " E.M., however, was in fine form and made the hit of the innings— a five."

" Directly after," the report goes on, " Jackson had an opportunity for Grace skied a ball. Jackson ran in to catch it but, finding he had gone too far, turned back and lost sight of the ball for, turning round twice, he completely missed it to the great delight and amusement of the spectators." Various stories are told about the height to which " E.M." sometimes skied that ball but, if reliance can be placed on this account, it must have been a phenomenal hit for the fielder appears to have run in, run back and turned round twice before the ball eventually came to earth.

After scoring 37, " E.M." was given out l.b.w. to Jackson but there followed a fine stand by Sewell and Danbery; 150 had been scored when young Gilbert came in at the fall of the seventh wicket. He had been given precedence in the batting over both Henry and Alfred and fully justified this move by scoring 32 before being bowled by Tinley, who a few years later distinguished himself by dismissing " W.G." for nought in both innings at Lansdown (this game, however, did not rank as first class). The innings of the XXII reached a total of 212, then came a sad response by the professionals, who were about to sail for Australia " to show the Colonials how the game of cricket should be played," as a contemporary reference states.

Failing entirely to cope with the bowling of E. M. Grace and
E. T. Daubney, the XI were all out for a paltry 86, the highest
scorer being the wicket-keeper, H. H. Stephenson, who carried
his bat for 18. Following on 126 runs behind, these famous
players did slightly better but even so their second innings
total of 106 left them the losers by an innings and 20 runs.
" E.M." was really the hero of the match for not only did he
make 37 but, with his fast round-arm deliveries, took five
wickets in each innings. E. T. Daubney with seven wickets
in the match also bowled well besides making 44, the highest
innings of the game, while Pillinger, it is recorded, kept wicket
admirably with the Rev. J. Mirehouse long-stopping in such
excellent style that there was only one bye in each innings.

As the result of his excellent all-round cricket in this game,
" E.M.," although only 21 years of age, received an invitation
to tour Australia with George Parr's team, which he accepted.
Here are the full scores of this historic match between XXII of
Bristol and District and the All-England XI:—

BRISTOL, 1st Innings.

E. M. GRACE, lbw, b Jackson	37
D. E. BERNARD, b Willsher	0
W. JONES, c Willsher, b Tarrant	10
J. D. B. TRENFIELD, st H. Stephenson, b Tinley	13
S. BRAMHALL (Capt. Rose), c Moore, b Jackson	7
E. A. HOWSON, b Jackson	0
J. SEWELL, c and b Tarrant	38
E. T. DAUBNEY, c Stephenson, b Jackson	44
J. ALLEN, b Tinley	3
W. G. GRACE, b Tinley	32
W. E. MIREHOUSE, c Tarrant, b Tinley	1
A. F. DAVIE, c Clarke, b Tinley	4
ALFRED GRACE, c Anderson, b Tinley	3
HENRY GRACE, b Jackson	0
J. F. FUSSELL, st H. Stephenson, b Tinley	1
W. PILLINGER, b Jackson	0
T. H. HILL, b Tinley	10
Rev. J. MIREHOUSE, c Anderson, b Tinley	2
R. BRUCE, b Jackson	0
—. SAVAGE, c Moore, b Jackson	0
—. BUDGE, st H. Stephenson, b Tinley	0
L. HARRIS, not out	1
Byes 2, leg-byes 4	6
	212

ALL-ENGLAND XI.

TARRANT, c Sewell, b Daubney	7	run out	7
WILLSHER, b E. M. Grace	11	c and b E. M. Grace	13
E. STEPHENSON, c W. G. Grace, b Daubney	7	c E. M. Grace, b W. G. Grace	11

HAYWARD, b Daubney	3	c Sub., b Daubney	5
W. H. MOORE, b E. M. Grace	8	b E. M. Grace	3
ANDERSON, b E. M. Grace	4	b Howson	6
CLARKE, c W. Mirehouse, b E. M. Grace	4	c Budge, b E. M. Grace	8
JULIUS CAESAR, b E. M. Grace	0	st Pillinger, b Daubney	5
H. H. STEPHENSON, not out	18	st Pillinger, b E. M. Grace	13
JACKSON, c and b Daubney	15	c Davie, b E. M. Grace	12
TINLEY, c Sewell, b Daubney	6	not out	17
Leg-bye 1, wides 2	3	Bye 1, wides 5	6
	86		**106**

Result: Bristol and District won by an innings and 20 runs.

It is, of course, very difficult now to appreciate the merit of the Bristol cricketers' performance in defeating this All-England XI, but it must have been a great achievement and indicated that apart from the members of the Grace family, there were some very fine players in the district. Another point that enhances their win was that the local team had to bat on what would nowadays be regarded as a very rough wicket even for a club game, besides which they were opposed to the best bowling in England. "Tarrant, Willsher and Jackson," stated W. G. Grace many years after, "that trio of bowlers were in the heyday of their strength. Tarrant, who played for Cambridgeshire, was generally known as ' Tear'em ' because he took such a long run before delivering the ball and gave himself the appearance of ferocity; his deliveries were very straight and very fast—as fast, if not faster, than Tom Richardson. Jackson also bowled at a great pace, while Willsher, a Kent man, was one of the most difficult left-handers I ever had to play against." Such were the memories " W.G." had in later life of the bowlers he had to meet that day on Durdham Downs.

In this game, as in others after round-arm bowling was introduced, the rules of the game forbade a bowler to raise his arm above his shoulder, and it was due to the number of times Willsher was no-balled for doing so that some years later this rule was altered. It was in this notable game on the Bristol Downs, too, that the rare sight of a man in the outfield was seen when " E.M." was batting, for " E.M." was the first batsman to go out to fast bowling and drive the ball high and far to long-on or long-off. There were no boundaries in those days and fielders had to dash through the ring of spectators when the ball went beyond them; it must have been a mighty hit off Tarrant, the fast bowler, which enabled " E.M." to run

five for the stroke.   The institution of boundaries, by the way,
came about in rather a curious fashion.   During a match at
Lord's, the ball was hit among the spectators and A. N.
(Monkey) Hornby of Lancashire, in dashing after it, knocked
over an old gentleman and injured him rather badly.   The
result of this unfortunate accident was that the authorities
decided to mark off a boundary line, their example being
followed by those in control of the other grounds.

A curious sequel to the All-England match on Durdham
Downs was a case of assault heard by the Bristol magistrates.
Then, as on various other occasions since, objection was raised
to the pitch being reserved for cricketers only, and the individual who raised this objection made himself such a nuisance
that he was unceremoniously bundled out of the way.   The
moving spirit in this affair seems to have been that gentleman,
Mr. Bramhall, who played in the game under the pseudonym
of " Captain Rose;" at any rate he had to answer the summons
for alleged assault.   The aggrieved party, however, obtained
little sympathy from the magistrates who, being evidently all
good sportsmen, dismissed the case which naturally provoked
a good deal of correspondence in the local papers.   One of
these letters is of special interest as it throws light on the date
the Clifton Club was granted the right to enclose a pitch on
the Downs.

> " Thirty-five years ago—1828—the Clifton Club," says
> the letter, " by leave of the lords of the manor enclosed a
> portion of the ground by the Sea-Walls, paying a trifle
> only to show it was by sufferance they held the ground,
> and again 16 years ago—1847—by leave of the lords they
> moved their pitch to the present position and at great
> expense they levelled and re-turned the ground."

This letter clears up a point that has often been discussed.

CHAPTER V.

Shortly after the match between Bristol and All-England, described in the last chapter, the defeated Professionals' team, including the triumphant " E.M.," left for Australia. Young Edward went forth on this great adventure with a very fine reputation, his record for the season of 1863 being the excellent one of : —

14 matches.   745 runs.   Top score 129.   Average 29.

In fact, the late W. W. Read says in his " Annals of Cricket " with reference to that year . . . " In the great matches of the year there are some Leviathan scores. Mr. E. M. Grace's, as usual at this time, were very prominent among them and some of his performances were remarkable exhibitions of what would be styled good cricket without being showy or affecting the least display."

Unfortunately he was not at all well when he arrived in Australia, which he attributed to the ship's diet which was not as it is to-day, also he was hampered by a whitlow on his finger which prevented him from doing himself justice. Consequently, although doing fairly well, he was unable to live up to the reputation he had made for himself at home. During his visit, however, he and Tarrant excited a great deal of interest by playing several single-wicket games, which they won easily. " E.M." did not return home with the rest of the team, preferring to holiday in Australia and, when he did arrive back in England, the summer was half over. His absence from this country, however, gave young Gilbert his first opportunity to play in a big match for, in company with his eldest brother Henry, he was invited to join the annual tour of the South Wales team.

An enterprising Cardiff sportsman was responsible for this annual cricket pilgrimage to London and elsewhere but South Wales was represented in little else than name. Nevertheless, the manager of this " scratch " team must figure in cricket history as the lucky individual who had the priviledge of bring-

ing " W.G." out. As I have already mentioned, Henry was
also a member of the team but, being merely a good average
club player and nothing more, there are no outstanding deeds
of his on the cricket field to record.

In the first match at Kennington Oval, " W.G.," being the
youngest member of the side, the South Wales captain did not
apparently treat him seriously as a batsman; at any rate he
sent him in low down on the list and Gilbert was out for 5.
In the second innings, however, when runs were badly needed,
young " W.G.," playing with skill, produced 38 runs. Despite
this promising effort and the fact that he also took 4 wickets,
" W.G." was informed that he would not be required for the
next match which was at Brighton; no doubt both captain
and manager of the team thought they would easily be able to
pick up a man on the spot to play against the Gentlemen of
Sussex. Henry, however, had other ideas on the subject and
protested: his young brother had been asked to take part in
the tour, not in one match and, as several other West of
England players were prepared to pack up and go if young
Gilbert was dropped, the captain was compelled to stand by
his bargain.

Going in first wicket down, this tall loose-limbed youth of
16 created a sensation by staying in until he had scored no
fewer than 170 runs, while in his second innings he was not
out 56. What the feelings of the South Wales captain were,
as " W.G." piled up runs by cricket the like of which had not
been seen since the death of the great Alfred Mynn, have not
been recorded but can be well imagined. Of course, after this
triumph, " W.G." was included in the XI which played the
M.C.C. at Lord's on the way home, and he signalised his
first appearance on this classic ground, upon which so many of
his later triumphs were to be achieved, by scoring 50. Included
in the South Wales team was Mr. J. J. Sewell, a fine cricketer,
being a hard hitting batsman and an excellent fielder in any
position but especially at cover point, and who had played
in the historic match on Durdham Downs the previous year.

Harking back a little to 1862, we find that the first inter-
county match in Bristol took place during that year between
Gloucestershire and Devonshire on Durdham Down. " E.M."
opened the innings with J. J. Sewell and together they put
on 113 runs for the first wicket, " E.M." scoring 57 and Sewell

65; Gloucestershire won by an innings and the local paper commented on the match as follows: —

" The County has made a good beginning and we hope they will long retain the laurels they have so gallantly won and, who knows but in time, they may be fit antagonists for Cambridge, Yorkshire, Kent and, even Surrey itself. It may appear presumptuous to speculate thus, but we believe there is plenty of good stuff in the district."

I append here the full scores of this initial county game in Bristol, which Gloucestershire won so handsomely, thanks to the all-round cricket of " E.M." who, in addition to scoring 57, took 13 wickets for 69 runs. Besides " E.M.," Henry and Alfred and " Uncle " Pocock played for the local county.

DEVONSHIRE.

S. BUDD, c Belcher, b H. Grace	15	c H. Grace, b Belcher	13
G. T. WARNER, c Belcher, b E. Grace	19	b E. M. Grace	7
SIMS, b H. Grace	1	b Belcher	0
R. S. BUDD, c Pocock, b E. M. Grace	0	b E. M. Grace	24
GILL, b E. M. Grace	7	c Butterworth, b E. Grace	1
HALBERTON, c Pocock, b E. M. Grace	0	st Gruning, b E. M. Grace	1
S. WARNER, b H. Grace	1	b E. M. Grace	6
REV. R. KINDERSLEY, c Gruning, b E. Grace	14	b E. M. Grace	3
MORRIS, c and b E. M. Grace	14	c and b Belcher	2
YEO, c E. Grace, b H. Grace	1	b E. M. Grace	0
ABRAHAM, not out	1	not out	0
Wides 2, byes 3, leg-bye 1	6	Wides 2, byes 3, leg-bye 1	6
	79		**63**

GLOUCESTERSHIRE.

E. M. GRACE, b S. Warner	57
J. J. SEWELL, c Sims, b S. Warner	65
BELCHER, b Gill	21
S. BRAMHALL, c Kindersley, b Abraham	8
A. POCOCK, b Gill	2
H. GRACE, b Gill	4
HILL, b Abraham	0
GRUNING, not out	19
A. GRACE, c Yeo, b Gill	7
BUTTERWORTH, b Morris	3
Hon. J. YARDE-BULLER, c G. Warner, b Halberton	3
Wides 20, byes 3, leg-byes 4, no balls 3	30
	219

While we are retracing our footsteps somewhat, there are two other games which figure in the early annals of Bristol cricket which I should like to mention, for we cannot attach too much importance to these early games for they laid the foundations of cricket's prestige in the West Country. It will perhaps surprise many of the young men of to-day that a lot of cricket was played by their grandfathers over eighty years ago, and some very interesting games too, as the newspapers of the period prove. A Saturday afternoon on Clifton Downs in summer time then was not very different from what it is to-day; there was just as keen a scramble after the best pitch and, no doubt, wrangles were more common than now. The young men of 1863, however, were unable to get to the Downs as easily as they can nowadays; in fact, I have come across a letter in the correspondence column of a Bristol newspaper of that time urging the omnibus proprietors to start a bus for the Downs from the Exchange at 2.30 p.m., so that cricketers and their friends may be on the Downs by 3 o'clock. The Graces figured in many club matches played on the Downs at this time; in one game " E.M." was in the Lansdown XI, while Henry, Alfred and "W.G." played for Clifton. In this particular match, sad to relate, " W.G." made a pair of spectacles, " E.M." getting him leg before in the first innings and clean bowling him in the second. The fact that he was bowling against his young brother, who was only 15 years old, made no difference to Edward Mills Grace, who all through his life played without the least sentiment; he was never known to play otherwise than cricket in the strictest sense; he gave no favours and expected none. All the same it was a joy to play with or against him, and hundreds of old cricketers in Bristol and district have had this pleasure at one time or another.

There is a report in one of the local papers of 1863 of a match between Portland and Somerset, which was also played on the Downs and resulted in Somerset being soundly beaten too by cricketers who were, no doubt, associated with Portland Chapel. In the same year a Carlton Club figured frequently in the cricket reports and it is interesting to come across the name of G. F. (Fred) Grace, then only in his thirteenth year, playing for Stapleton against Hanham. In 1865 a very interesting match was played at Bath between XVIII of the Lansdown Club and the United All-England XI; the local team including no fewer than three of the Grace family—" E.M.," Henry and " W.G." The XVIII won easily by an innings, thanks to a splendid knock of 121 by " E.M." and fine bowling by all three of the brothers Grace, who took all the wickets between them, putting out the powerful All-England XI for 99 and 87. One hit of " E.M.'s " went into the river; he was eventually caught, however, at long-leg by G. M. Kelson, the Kent amateur. " E.M.'s " innings was all the more creditable as at that time such an achievement against the All-England XI was almost unheard of.

During 1865 " W.G." accomplished what was so far his best bowling performance; he and Mr. I. D. Walker (one of the famous Walkers of Southgate) playing for the Gentlemen of the South against the Players of the South at Kennington Oval took all the wickets between them " W.G.'s " share being 13 (8 in the second innings) and Walker's 7. " E.M." was unable to play owing to ill-health.

It was on this ground too in the September, during the match between XVIII of the Gentlemen of the South and the United South of England XI, that " E.M." was involved in an accident which at one time threatened to be serious. Jupp, a noted stonewaller, was batting and the bowlers, having tried unsuccessfully to remove him, were wondering how to get him out. Both " E.M." and I. D. Walker had tried in vain, then " E.M." said—" I'll give him a high toss " and he did. He bowled a high underhand ball which, soaring right over Jupp's head, fell on the top of the wicket, removing the bail. This caused considerable sensation; spectators expressed their feelings freely and it soon looked as if there was going to be a riot. Some called to Jupp to go out and it appeared that blows between the onlookers and the players were imminent; in fact, several of the Gentlemen pulled up stumps with which to defend themselves, if necessary. The game was then suspended for a little while until the troubled waters had been calmed and the innings could be resumed.

As it was the custom of the Surrey Club in the 60's to present a bat to any player who scored 50 runs in an innings at the Oval, " E.M.," who in this memorable match made 64 and 56, received two bats, which brought the total of bats presented to him at that time to 75. For the season of 1865 " E.M." averaged nearly 40 runs per innings for 18 innings.

The first link in the chain of " W.G.'s " centuries in first-class cricket was forged at the Oval on the last two days of July, 1866; the match was England versus Surrey and young Gilbert, who had just passed his eighteenth birthday and was playing for the former team, went in when the third wicket had fallen for 96. Surrey had good bowlers then as in later years but " W.G.," playing superb cricket, scored no less than 224 runs and was still undefeated when the last wicket fell with the total at 521. No such score had ever been made at the Oval before and it was said that the cheering, when he returned to the pavillion, could be heard as far away as Mr. Spurgeon's Tabernacle. This was the game in which " W.G." was allowed off on the third day in order to compete in the sports at the Crystal Palace and, as it has now become historic, I append England's score below: —

ENGLAND.

Dr. E. M. GRACE, c Jupp, b Humphrey	9
C. PAYNE, b Griffith	86
G. WOOTTON, b Jupp	19
T. HEARNE, c and b Jupp	19
W. G. GRACE, not out	224
C. COWARD, b Humphrey	9
G. BENNETT, c Griffith, b Humphrey	4
V. E. WALKER, c Jupp, b Noble	54
JAS. LILLYWHITE, Jnr., b Jupp	32
T. ROUND, b Miller	42
E. WILLSHER, c Miller, b Noble	9
Extras	14
	521

A month later " W.G." was again on the Oval, this time playing for the Gentlemen of the South against the Players of the South. Gate receipts being probably as important in 1866 as in 1948, a young man who had beaten all batting records at the Oval a month earlier, was bound to be a great attraction and, being once again in wonderful all-round form, he scored 173 not out as well as taking 7 wickets for 92 in the first innings and 2 for 16 in the second. Thus, in two innings on this ground, young Gilbert had scored 397 runs without losing his wicket on either occasion, and it is worth remembering that at this time there were still no boundaries, every hit had to be run for and his innings included several sixes. Two of these big hits were made in his second large score with a new bat presented to him by the Surrey Club in recognition of his 224 not out for England the previous month. The great impression that his batting made upon the critics is shown by the following extract from " Bell's Life ": —

> " This young gentleman's performances during the season have been extraordinary, and his 224 (not out) at the Oval in the match Surrey v. England, and his 173 (not out) in the Gentlemen of the South v. the Players of the South will long be remembered in cricketing circles."

To those of us who cherish memories of the Grand Old Man of Cricket, he was a bowler of soft-looking stuff; we remember him ambling up to the wicket, delivering the ball with an action that was neither round nor over-arm but something between the two, and the following up wide on the off-side.   As a young man he bowled at average medium pace but was noted for his dexterity in fielding to his own bowling.

> " The moment he had delivered the ball," wrote the late Lord Harris some years ago, " he took so much ground to the left as to be himself extra mid-off, and he never funked a return, however hard and low it came.   I have seen him make some extraordinary catches thus."

This habit of making ground to the left he maintained throughout his cricket career and many old cricketers will remember fielding just behind him to stop the straight drive.

In addition to big cricket, " W.G." managed to get in some local games as well during 1866 but, curiously enough, he was never quite such a terror to club bowlers as was his brother " E.M."; nevertheless, he made 157 and 150 not out for Clifton, and 101 for Bedminster.   One word more about 1866: it was during this year that " W.G." played his first game at Sheffield when he captained XVIII Colts of Nottingham and Sheffield against An England XI. " E.M." was originally chosen to lead the local side but was unable to do so and appointed his young brother as his deputy: he made 9 and 36.

1867 was not a good year for " W.G." for, although taking over 100 wickets, he failed to register a single century; it should, however, be stated in extenuation of this that he suffered from scarlet fever during the summer, which naturally left its mark upon his batting.

Towards the end of the '60's, the youngest of the brothers Grace—G.F. or Fred, as he was usually known, came into prominence. He had displayed much skill as a boy and in local games had frequently made a hundred while quite a youngster.

At the early age of nine he performed an amazing bowling feat,
taking 13 wickets in a match against grown-up men. He made
his debut in first-class cricket by playing for the North of
the Thames v. the South of the Thames at Canterbury, while
two years later he made his initial appearance at Lord's for
England versus the M.C.C. and Ground. In this game "W.G."
and "G.F." were in the England XI, while " E.M." represented
the M.C.C.

A question that has often arisen but which will never be
really satisfactorily answered is " Which of the Champion's 126
centuries was his best display of batting?" In the Doctor's
own opinion, one of his best innings in first-class cricket was
his first hundred for the Gentlemen against the Players at
Lord's in 1868. About this time the pitch at H.Q. was
notoriously bad; in fact, one of the worst in the country upon
which important was played. Yet " W.G.," who was not yet
twenty, overcame all the difficulties of dealing with " shooters "
as well as balls that flew over the wicket-keeper's head and
kept Mortlock, the long-stop, busy, and scored 134 out of a
total of 201, being undefeated at the close. His hits, which
included one 6, two 5s, eleven 4s and nine 3s all run out,
indicate the sort of cricket which " W.G." provided for the
spectators on that memorable occasion. The next highest score
of the match was 28 by B. Cooper, who in the following year
was concerned with " W.G." in a first wicket stand of 283,
which remained a record for many years, but no other member
of the Gentlemen's team reached double figures. The Players
were hopelessly outplayed and soundly beaten for not only
were they unable to get young Gilbert out but they were
equally unable to play his bowling and in the two innings he
took 10 wickets at a very small cost. This was " W.G.'s "
second appearance for the Gentlemen; he had made his debut
in this classic fixture in June, 1865, when by scoring 34 out of
77 in the second innings, he helped the Amateurs to beat the
Professionals for the first time in 19 successive games. For
many years afterwards he dominated this great game at Lord's
and during the next 20 years, thanks to the Doctor they lost
two matches at Head-quarters. " Never before or since "
wrote the Rev. R. S. Holmes some years later " in cricket or
any other sport has one man played so overwhelming a part."
It is a happy memory to me that I saw every ball bowled in
" W.G.'s " Jubilee Match at Lord's for the Gentlemen in 1898,

and I still treasure a permit he wrote me giving access to the Pavilion—a very great privilege.

Returning to the Gentlemen v. Players match at Lord's in 1868, it is worth mentioning that " E.M." bowled both round-arm and lobs while the Players were batting. Every middle-aged cricketer in Bristol knew " E.M." and his famous lob, but very few remember him as a fast round-arm bowler. I remember asking him one day, when we were sitting in the pavilion at the County Ground, Bristol, waiting for the rain to clear off, when he first started bowling underhand " diddlers." He replied that he had been bowling lobs since the early 60's. In one of his many games for Lansdown, which sometimes involved a 9 miles walk to the ground and another 9 miles home again after the game, the home team couldn't get their opponents out. " Ever bowl lobs?" asked the Lansdown captain. " No, but I'll have a try " answered " E.M."; and he did, capturing seven wickets. From that time his round-arm deliveries were introduced but occasionally and sometimes unexpectedly in the course of an over, much to the discomfiture of the batsman.

When in 1868 " W.G." scored 130 in the first innings and 104 not out in the second, for South of the Thames v. North of the Thames at Canterbury, he accomplished a batting feat which had only been performed once before. The first cricketer to score a century in each innings of a match was William Lambert who, as far back as 1817, made 107 not out and 157 in a game at Lord's. A remarkable feature of " W.G.'s " performance was that in spite of his efforts, he was on the losing side. It was in this game that " G.F." made his first appearance in big cricket.

May 14th, 1869, marked young Gilbert's debut for the M.C.C., to which august body he had just previously been elected a member; and he celebrated his inclusion in the Club side by scoring 117. In his first season for the M.C.C., " W.G." had a very fine all-round record, scoring 724 runs in 12 innings for an average of 60, as well as taking 44 wickets at a cost of 12 runs apiece. His best score in all first-class games in 1869 was his 180 for the Gentlemen of the South v. the Players of the South at the Oval; in this particular match the Gentlemen went in facing a first innings of 475, but " W.G." and B. B. Cooper, the old Rugby captain, opened with the record partnership of 283, defying the Players' bowling for 3¾ hours,—

Cooper making 101, and the Amateurs actually headed the Professionals' total by 78.   Altogether during that season, "W.G." scored 6 centuries in first-class matches, the other 5 being made against Surrey, Kent, Notts and Oxford University (for the M.C.C.) and South v. North.

Thus ended the Sixties—that wonderful decade which saw the rise not only of "E.M." Grace but of "W.G." and "G.F." too; in all probability the most remarkable brotherhood in the history of any sport.

CHAPTER VI.

Having traced the history of the Grace family as far as the end of the Sixties, let us forget for the moment all about them as cricketers and follow their careers in other spheres of sport, both in Bristol and elsewhere. Old friends who shared their boyhood pastimes with the Graces at Downend have told me that in their games " W.G." was never considered much of a runner; yet he, however, had a fancy as a youth of sixteen to excel in this branch of sport as well as cricket. So keen, in fact, was he on running that he eventually became the best man of his day over hurdles and for a season the best 100 yards man in England, through sheer grit and perseverance. It is said that his ambition in this respect was fired through winning the Strangers' Race at the Clifton College sports for, attending in 1866 (four years after the school was opened), he heard that there was an event open to visitors, entered and won it. But for this chance success he would probably have contented himself with cricket; having, however, found a new outlet for his abounding vitality, he proceeded to develop it. In that year he missed no chance of making entries at sports' meetings in the district and anything for which he was eligible found him an enthusiastic competitor.

Long before the Oakfield Rugby Club came into existence— the club that gave (not always willingly) several good players to Bristol, including Edward Fenner—there was an Oakfield Cricket Club and at their annual sports " W.G." won the 200 yards hurdles, the 300 yards flat, the ladies' prize for 440 yards, and throwing the cricket ball (105 yards). At the Long Ashton sports Grace had five firsts, including the all-comers 440 yards, and the hop, step and jump event. His most notable success that year, however, was the 440 yards hurdle race at the National Olympian Association Meeting which took place at the Crystal Palace on August 1st. " W.G." had been playing for England against Surrey at the Oval—a memorable day in his career for he had scored 224 not out, his first hundred in first-class cricket; the match was not over but " W.G.," having explained to his capain, V. E. Walker, that he wished to compete at the Crystal Palace, was allowed to leave and thus enjoyed the wonderful experience of scoring a not out double century for England and winning a national hurdle race, all within three days. It would be interesting to know what the present England captain would think of a request from a member of his team to be allowed off on the third day to take part in a hurdles race at a sports meeting. Dr. Grace, discussing the matter years afterwards, said: " I know what I should say if such a request were made to me but I'm afraid the remark wouldn't look very pretty in print'"

There were not so many sporting diversions in the Sixties as there are now—golf and lawn tennis were almost unknown; bowls was to the majority of people in Bristol a game that had something to do with Drake and the Spaniards. Apart from cricket, athletic sports were the outstanding events of the summer and these attracted widespread interest. Running matches on the main road were frequent events and many are recorded in the newspapers of eighty odd years ago, usually promoted by the landlord of some popular public house, the stakes varying from £2 to £10. Coronation Road, Bedminster, seems to have been a favourite course for these matches and newspaper reports indicate that bookmakers were usually busy taking bets from the rival factions. The Zoological Gardens, Clifton, was for many years the only place in the district where events on a big scale could be held, and both " W.G." and " E.M." were frequent competitors there. The leading event of the year was the Bristol, Clifton and West of England Athletic Festival and, in the season we are discussing, 1866— " W.G." had the satisfaction of winning the gold medal for the biggest number of successes; his record was 4 firsts and 2 seconds. " E.M." beat his younger brother in the 200 yards race but was defeated after a terrific sprint by " W.G." in the 100 yards, Gilbert having gained 2 yards by beating the pistol.

Members of the Bedminster Cricket Club will be interested to know that their predecessors regularly organised an important athletic meeting at the Clifton Zoo. Indeed, it is both illuminating and somewhat puzzling to find, on going into sporting history of Bristol, how prominently Bedminster has figured in this phase of life in the City. In the early Sixties, a good part of the area now covered by houses and factories was entirely rural, yet here flourished one of our earliest cricket

DR. W. G. GRACE

clubs and here also was formed the first Rugby football club in Bristol—" W.G." played his only games of rugger on the field behind the " Hen and Chickens " hostelry. " E.M." joined the Bedminster Cricket Club as early as 1857 and remained a member for a great many years, and it was at the Bedminster Club sports at the Clifton Zoo in 1867 that Mr. W. Hayes Olive beat " W.G." in the 100 yard race. " Uncle Bill," as Mr. Olive was affectionately called by his intimate friends, was nearing his ninetieth birthday, was almost as upright now as on that memorable occasion when he covered the 100 yards in 10½ seconds. leaving " W.G." to come in third. The Graces (" E.M." and " W.G."), however, as usual carried off many of the prizes, " E.M." being the more successful of the two. His successes included the long jump with 19ft. 3ins.; the high jump and the hurdle race in which " W.G." was second. The account of this athletic meeting which appeared in the " Western Daily Press " suggests that the management was not all that could be desired :

> " There were too many masters " it states. " Everybody who had any connection, however remote, with the club thought he had the right to have a voice in all cases of disputes and indeed some who had nothing to do with the club at all were the noisiest in interfering. The stewards seemed utterly useless for the purpose of keeping the roped-in space clear, and in consequence those who had business were hindered by the presence of those who had not. In any further sports this club may promote, it will be well for them to adopt a stringent regulation (and carry it out) as to the keeping of the ground."

The handicapping of 81 years ago seems to have been done in a haphazard way for the report states :—

> " The handicapping gave mortal offence to a few although, considering the difficulty under which he laboured, Mr. Jones discharged his thankless task remarkably well. But we must mention that the whole system of handicapping as hitherto carried out in Bristol is a mistake. It was obvious on Saturday that many men had a greater start than they were entitled to, while others were placed in the rear without any claim for such placing. It is impossible to have a fair handicapping unless the entries are closed two or three days before the race. We are aware that objections will be raised to this

view. Handicappers will tell us that they do not know
the men and without seeing them it is impossible to form
an estimate of their powers. But this is a mistake.
Men are judged too much by their appearance and, not
a little, by their own powers of persuasion. There is a
great deal too much talking to and interfering with the
handicapper. The same remark applies to the umpire. In
one race we heard a competitor tell Mr. Peter Adams that
if it was run in heats he would not start, while half-a-
dozen others protested in exactly the opposite direction."

One wonders what promoters of athletic gatherings in these
enlightened days would think if their management was subject
to such outspoken criticism.

During 1867 and 1868, " W.G." was studying at the Bristol
Medical School and had less time to spare for sport but, even
so, his successes included firsts at the London Athletic Club
Meeting, the Blackheath Sports and at the Bedminster Club
Sports in 1868—four firsts. His best season, however, was
1869 when his record for entries at Oxford University, the
Amateur Athletic Club Championships, the London Athletic
Club Meeting, the Merchant Taylors' School sports, Bristol
and Clifton Athletic Festival, the Cheltenham Sports meeting at
Montepellier Gardens, the Bedminster Cricket Club sports, the
Clifton Zoological Gardens Sports meeting, and the Oval,
London, was seventeen firsts and nine seconds. He was scratch
man at the Bedminster Club sports that year but won three
firsts, two seconds and the gold medal for the highest number
of wins. " W.G." ran in a few meetings in 1870 but his track
career ended. His best times were:

100 yards on grass ...	...	10 4-5 secs.
150 yards (5 yds. start)	...	15½ secs.
200 yards hurdle race	...	28 secs.
440 yards flat race ...	...	52 1-5 secs.
Long jump	...	17½ ft.
High jump	...	5 ft.
Hop, step and a jump	...	41 ft.
Pole leap	...	9 ft.
Throwing the cricket ball	...	117 yards

In judging W. G. Grace's form in this branch of sport, it
must be remembered that he was busy preparing to be a doctor
and just as busy qualifying for the title of " Champion

Cricketer of the World for all time "; therefore he could not have had much time to carry out the intensive training so necessary for foot racing and his records, in these circumstances, are wonderful.

Rugby football at this time was beginning to make its appeal all over the country to stouthearted young fellows. Blackheath, Richmond, Harlequins, Liverpool, Manchester and other noted clubs all came into existence during the Sixties, as also did the Bedminster (Bristol) R.F.C. which remained the only Rugger club in Bristol until the formation of the Clifton Club in 1872. There were until quite recently two survivors of Bristol's first Rugby football club — the late Mr. W. H. Brown and Mr. R. E. Bush, whose brother " J.A.," the giant wicket-keeper, toured Australia with " W.G." in 1873—both of whom could recall W. G. Grace playing football in the old " Hen and Chickens " field. Mr. Brown, who for many years was the esteemed President of the Bristol Cricket Association, was one of the best all-round athletes in Bristol and for the kind of rugger they played over sixty years ago, he was generously endowed physically. In one match " W.G." was on the other side and there came a turn in the tide of the game when a young giant, well over 6 feet tall and weighing over 12 stone, had to be stopped: and he was. The two came together with a mighty crash; then one got up and staggered about until the shock had passed. The other, " W.G.," however, took longer to recover and apparently his first thought, when mind and body were again normal, was that Rugby football was not the game to follow if accidents, which might interfere with cricket, were to be avoided. At any rate that is the last occasion known to his contemporaries upon which W. G. Grace took part in a game of rugger. There is no record of any other member of the Grace family playing football but it may be taken for granted that " W.G.," with his magnificent physique, would have excelled at this vigorous sport if he had not been so keen on keeping fit and sound in wind and limb for the game in which his name will always be associated as long as the word " Cricket " has a meaning to the youth of the Empire.

Before I pass on to the doings of the Graces in the Seventies, I must allude to two rather interesting matches in which they took part in the late Sixties. The first was played at Lord's in June 1868 between the M.C.C. and the Gentlemen of Gloucestershire, the latter winning by 131 runs. The visiting team, including the three Graces—and it can honestly be said that the victory was due to their combined efforts for "E.M." in addition to scoring 65 in the second innings, claimed 12 wickets in the match and also caught an opponent; " W.G." made 24 and 13, took 5 wickets and caught one, while the youngest brother Fred (G.F.), although scoring only 3 and 2, caught out two of the M.C.C. batsmen. In the second game between XX of Clifton and the United All-England XI, which took place on the Clifton College Ground in July, 1868, no fewer than four Graces appeared in the local team, Henry being the additional member of the family. On this occasion, however, they were on the losing side, being entirely unable to cope with the bowling of Tarrant and Tom Emmett, who took all the wickets between them, while the two famous bats-men, T. Hayward (father of the future Surrey crack) and Car-penter scored 82 not out and 36 respectively. The local side included several notable names in addition to the Graces, for there was T. G. Matthews, who died some years ago at a great age and who scored 201 for Gloucestershire against Surrey on the same ground in 1871; Frank Townsend, the father of that brilliant all-rounder C. L. (Charlie) Townsend and grand-father of the old Oxford Blue, D. C. H. Townsend, who made 193 for Oxford in the 'Varsity match of 1934. Then there was E. F. S. Tylecote, who had scored 404 in a game while at Clifton College and who afterwards captained Oxford and played for Kent. Lastly there was J. A. Bush, whom we have already mentioned. It is worth noting that " W.G." with scores of 26 in each innings was the only member of the team who could stand up to the bowling of Tarrant and Emmett.

It was in Gloucestershire's match against the M.C.C. at Lord's in 1868 that the first professional appeared in the West Country team, one W. H. Hall, the predecessor of that band of fine professionals who have so loyally served the club. Where Hall hailed from is not recorded, neither is it stated in the published reference to this game whether he was a batsman or a bowler; in any case he does not appear to have helped materially in the memorable victory for his two innings produced only 7 runs, while " E.M." and " W.G." took all the wickets.

CHAPTER VII

The question will probably occur to many of those who read this book—What sort of bowling had " W.G." and his brothers to face when knocking up their big scores? Comparison with bowlers of to-day is, of course, impossible; but it is generally asserted by accredited veteran witnesses, long enough associated with the game as players and spectators, to remember the great bowlers of the '60s and 30 years later—that at no period was the general standard higher than when " W.G." was a young man, achieving such feats of batting as the game had never before known. It must also always be remembered that very few of the pitches upon which the Graces had to play were comparable with the artificially prepared pitches of the last 40 years. Lord's, for instance, where the Champion gained so many of his early triumphs, was the most dangerous ground in England between 1869 and 1870. Indeed, during a match there in the latter season, Summers, a young Notts professional, was killed by a blow on the head from a rising ball. Fortunately, however, such fatalities as this have been rare in the history of the game but further evidence of the dangerous wickets on this particular ground is given by George Freeman, one of the greatest of Yorkshire bowlers, who wrote the following concerning an innings of 66, which " W.G." played for the M.C.C. against Yorkshire at Lord's in 1870:—

" A more wonderful innings was never played. Tom Emmett and I have often said it was a marvel the Doctor was not either maimed or unnerved for the rest of his days or killed outright. I often think of his pluck on that day when I watch a modern batsman scared if a medium ball hits him on the hand. He should have seen our expresses flying about his (" W.G.'s") head, ribs and shoulders in 1870."

Another great Yorkshire bowler, Allen Hill, has related that he had known the inside of " W.G.'s " thigh above the pad pounded into the appearance of a " mutton chop " by balls from George Freeman, which whipped in and struck the Champion.

From the time he was but a youth in his 'teens, " W.G." had had to stand up to fast bowlers, notably " Tear'em Tarrant " whom he regarded as faster than Tom Richardson and Edgar Willsher of Kent, a fast left-hander who is credited with being one of the most difficult bowlers the Doctor ever played against. John Jackson of Notts, a worthy forerunner of Harold Larwood, was also of the period when young Gilbert Grace was building up his reputation and he had to face them on pitches much less reliable than the average club wicket to-day.

In the Seventies came the Prince of bowlers, Alfred Shaw, who during his long and honourable career captured 1,900 wickets at an average cost of $11\frac{1}{2}$ runs each and who has never been surpassed as a master of length and artifice. His amazing performances included doing the " Hat-Trick " twice for Notts against Gloucestershire at Bristol in 1884. Years ago, when Alfred Shaw had passed from active participation in the game and was one of the most reliable umpires, I had the pleasure of meeting him on many occasions. Like all old cricketers, his regard for " W.G." amounted almost to veneration and he was exceedingly proud of the fact that he had bowled the Champion more times—21—than any other man in first-class cricket.

Just over 60 years ago, a Lancashire bowler named Cross-land, exploited the " Body-Line " theory, which raised such a storm of controversy in Australia in 1932-1933. At the Oval there was a scene—almost a riot—as the result of Cross-land's tactics and the newspapers of the period made almost as much fuss about it as did the modern journalists when the Australians raised their protests against Larwood's bowling on that tour. From the Oval, the Lancashire team travelled to Clifton to meet Gloucestershire and in the first over Cross-land bowled a ball which just missed " W.G.'s" head. Instantly there was a roar of protest from the spectators. " W.G.," however, would have none of it and, leaving the wicket, he walked over to the noisiest section of the crowd, told them that he would have the ground cleared if there were any more demonstrations and then proceeded to hit the Lancashire terror all over the field until he had scored 112.

The better the bowling, the better "W.G." batted; Lord Hawke has borne testimony to that feature of the great man's genius : —

> "He generally seemed to love the Yorkshire bowling and I think that was because our bowling was just a bit better, very often, than others he had to play. We possessed a succession of wonderful left-handers bowlers and I always thought that "W.G." played left-handed bowling more easily than right-handed. Personally I never saw two finer efforts than his two centuries against us at Clifton in 1888. He hit the very first ball for 4 plumb in the middle of the bat, and I felt we were out for a real leather-hunt. He never looked like being out. If George Hirst never bowled him, as he relates, Bobby Peel only did so on six occasions and Peate on nine, and they must have opposed him a number of times."

All the evidence of eminent cricketers and judges is in the direction of the bowling from which W. G. Grace gained the only title of "Champion" ever conferred by unanimous opinion upon a cricketer, being equal in variety and effectiveness to any that has been produced at any period in the history of the game.

All who remember Dr. W. G. Grace as a youth agree that he was very good looking but not quite so strikingly handsome as his brother Fred. Fortunately there are photographs and pictures of "W.G." at various stages in his progress to manhood but it is doubtful whether any of them would appeal to the modern young lady's idea of manly good looks for standards have changed in this as in other ways since Victorian times. In one of the many books dealing with the life of "W.G.," it is stated that a print exists showing a group of players at the Canterbury Festival in the '70s and that young Gilbert appears clean shaven. In every other picture of him about that period his aspect suggests that he followed the fashion of the time, cultivating the beard which in after years became so much a part of his personality and through which, according to the yarns of old stagers, the ball used to "whistle" on bumpy pitches. "I can clearly recall his physical characteristics when I first saw him in the Gentlemen and Players match in 1865," wrote Lord Cobham. "He was a tall loose-limbed lean boy and in marked contrast to his brother "E.M.," quite and shy in manner. He looked older than he was and indications of the beard which subsequently distinguished him through life were even then apparent. His fielding in the outfield during the early part of his career impressed me if anything more than his batting or bowling, for he was a beautiful thrower. He could run like a deer and had a very safe pair of hands. As a saver of runs he was unsurpassed." What a difference to the "W.G." whom we of a later generation saw for so many years fielding at point and rarely moving except to cross over or take a turn at bowling.

It is on record that about the time he had made a brilliant debut for the Marylebone Club persistent endeavours were made to get him to go up to Oxford and the late Canon E. E. Carter, a fine cricketer for Yorkshire in the early Seventies, stated in his reminiscences of the Champion that he tried his hardest to persuade him to go up to Oxford as an undergraduate, but his father would not allow him to sacrifice the time from his medical studies.

The year 1870 was a notable one for Gloucestershire cricket for it was then that the County Club, in a properly organised condition, opened to a long and honourable career with a match against Surrey on Durdham Downs, Clifton. There had, of course, been games of a semi-county nature for many years; the games against the All-England XI have already been mentioned, while in 1858 the Gentlemen of Gloucestershire played the I. Zingari in the park at Badminton and E. M. Grace, then only sixteen years old, had scored 25 and taken 6 wickets with his fast round-arm bowling. Dr. Henry Mills Grace was a man of vision as well as being a practical and enthusiastic cricketer and did his utmost to bring Gloucestershire into line with Surrey, Kent, Yorkshire and Sussex, where the county principle had for many years been recognised. Leading Gloucestershire sportsmen, however, failed to give him the necessary financial backing and occassional game were the only opportunities of testing the cricket resources of the county. During 1869, while young Gilbert was engaged in creating sensation after sensation by his wonderful feats with bat and ball, his father was busy laying the foundations of the Gloucestershire County Cricket Club on a firm and lasting basis and on June 2nd,· 1870, there commenced on Durdham Down the first official county match against Surrey. The home team, which included "E.M.," "W.G.," and Fred

Grace, won a low scoring game by 51 runs, and for this victory in their opening match were indebted to " W.G." who, besides scoring 26 and 25, took 9 wickets in the match for 96 runs, and also to Fred who made 16 and 15 and had 7 wickets for 86. C. R. Filgate, who was not out for 46 in the second innings, was top scorer for Gloucestershire, while R. Fenton Miles took the other four Surrey wickets for 24 runs. For Surrey the outstanding performances were Southerton's bowling 14 wickets in the match, including 9 for 67 in the second innings, and Jupp's batting—50 not out—also in the second innings.

A return match was played at Kennington Oval on July 28th and 29th, resulting this time in an even more convincing win for the Western county who beat Surrey in two days by an innings and 139 runs, despite the fact that E. M. Grace was unable to play. As in the previous game " W.G.," displaying wonderful all-round form, opened the innings and scored 143 runs; then after taking four wickets for 35 in Surrey's first innings, he and R. F. Miles bowling unchanged, proceeded to dismiss their opponents for a mere 46 runs. " W.G.'s " figures were 4 for 20 and Miles' 6 for 20, making the latter's record for the match 12 wickets for 106. Besides " W.G.'s " century the best batting on the side was Frank Townsend's 89 and Fred's 33. The full scores of the two matches are as follows : —

GLOUCESTERSHIRE v. SURREY,
played on Durdham Down, Bristol.

GLOUCESTERSHIRE

E. M. GRACE, c Southerton, b Street	2	c and b Vince	18
W. G. GRACE, c Pooley, b Southerton ..	26	c Pooley, b Southerton	25
T. G. MATTHEWS, c Street, b Southerton	5	c Mayo, b Southerton	7
F. TOWNSEND, b Street	11	c Pooley, b Southerton	20
G. F. GRACE, hit-wkt., b Southerton	16	c Griffith, b Southerton	15
J. HALFORD, lbw, b Street	6	hit-wkt., b Southerton	2
C. R. FILGATE, c Griffith, b Street	15	not out	48
J. MILLS, c Pooley, b Southerton	15	c Pooley, b Southerton	2
J. A. BUSH, not out	3	c T. Humphrey, b Southerton	14
R. F. MILES, run out	0	b Southerton	8
W. D. MACPHERSON, c Street, b Southerton	2	b Southerton	5
Byes 3, leg-byes 2	5	Byes 2, leg-bye 1	3
	106		167

SURREY

T. HUMPHREY, c Halford, b W. G. Grace	1	b G. F. Grace 5
JUPP, c E. M. Grace, b W. G. Grace	14	not out 50
E. POOLEY, c Filgate, b W. G. Grace	10	c and b G. F. Grace 8
BROWN, c Filgate, b W. G. Grace	3	c E. M. Grace, b G. F. Grace 3
H. H. STEPHENSON, b G. F. Grace	4	b W. G. Grace 0
R. HUMPHREY, c and b W. G. Grace ..	5	c E. M. Grace, b W. G. Grace 1
G. GRIFFITH, not out	41	c W. G. Grace, b Mills 5
J. STREET, b G. F. Grace	4	b Miles 5
H. MAYO, c E. M. Grace, b G. F. Grace	15	b G. F. Grace 4
VINCE, b G. F. Grace	1	c G. F. Grace, b Miles 0
J. SOUTHERTON, st Halford, b Miles ..	26	b Miles 0
Byes 7, leg-byes 2, wide 1	10	Byes 3, leg-bye 1, wides 3 7
	134	**88**

Result: Gloucestershire won by 51 runs.

SURREY v. GLOUCESTERSHIRE, at Kennington Oval.

GLOUCESTERSHIRE

W. G. GRACE, c Jupp, b Southerton	143
C. GORDON, st Pooley, b Street	0
F. TOWNSEND, c Rogers, b Griffith	89
G. F. GRACE, c Humphrey, b Southerton	33
G. STRACHAN, b Street	11
R. F. MILES, b Street	3
J. A. BUSH, not out	19
J. HALFORD, c Howell, b Southerton	0
J. J. CROSS, run out	0
A. MASTER, b Southerton	5
E. S. MORRIS, lbw, b Griffith	17
Byes 12, leg-byes 4, wides 2	18
	338

SURREY

JUPP, c Miles, b W. G. Grace	48	c Halford, b Miles 3
T. HUMPHREY, c Master, b Miles	29	st Bush, b Miles 5
E. POOLEY, b W. G. Grace	32	c G. F. Grace, b Miles 3
L. HOWELL, c G. F. Grace, b W. G. Grace	13	c Halford, b W. G. Grace .. 0
R. HUMPHREY, st Miles	6	b W. G. Grace 3
GRIFFITH, c Master, b W. G. Grace ..	17	st Bush, b Miles 0
G. BRAY, c Bush, b Miles	2	b Miles 4
STEPHENSON, st Bush, b Miles	1	st Bush, b Miles 7
G. ROGERS, not out	4	b W. G. Grace 0
STREET, st Bush, b Miles	4	c and b W. G. Grace 0
J. SOUTHERTON, b Miles	0	not out 15
Byes 4, leg-byes 2, wide 1	7	Byes 5, wide 1 6
	163	**46**

Result: Gloucestershire won by an innings and 129 runs.

In the latter match it is worth noting that J. A. Bush, the wicket-keeper, stumped four and caught two.

The only other first-class game in which Gloucestershire took part during 1870 was against the M.C.C. at Lord's and once again, thanks to the brilliant all-round form of " W.G.," the Westerners won by an innings and 88 runs. " W.G.," who opened the innings with C. S. Gordon, scored 172 out of a total of 276, a feat which he followed up by helping to put the Marylebone Club out for 76, he and Miles bowling unchanged. In the second innings he took 4 wickets for 27, his figures for the game being 7 for 65. The same year, playing for the Gentlemen of the South against the Gentlemen of the North, Fred Grace scored a brilliant 189 not out which, as " W.G." tells in his reminiscences, quite overshadowed his elder brother's (" W.G.'s ") 79.

For the Gentlemen against the Players that year " W.G." enjoyed a great success with 215 at the Oval and 109 at Lord's, in which game Fred made his first appearance for the Amateurs. " W.G.'s " fifth and last century in 1870 was his 117 not out for the M.C.C. against Notts, at Lord's, the unfortunate match in which young Summers received the fatal blow on the head from a bumping ball.

1871 brought further successes to Gloucestershire for, extending their programme, they beat the M.C.C. by five wickets, Surrey twice by an innings and drew and lost with Notts. At the Oval, E. M. Grace was mainly responsible for their victory, taking 9 wickets for 53 runs, while in the return game on the Clifton College Ground the honours went to T. G. Matthews who made 201, and Fred who scored 89. In the drawn game with Notts at Clifton, the Graces were well to the fore, " W.G." with 78 and 55, " E.M." wih 65, and young Fred with 46 not out. At Trent Bridge, it was no fault of the Champion's that the visitors lost by 10 wickets, for he followed up 79 in the first innings with 116 in the second. The following year, " W.G." was unable to play against Notts at Clifton, but both " E.M." and " G.F." gave excellent displays of batting, each scoring a century in the first innings—" E.M." 108; Fred not out 117. In the second innings, " E.M." was dismissed for 10, but at the end of the match Fred was still undefeated with 72 to his credit.

That Gloucestershire beat Yorkshire at Sheffield by an innings in 1872 was due almost entirely to the brothers Grace, for " W.G." was in his finest form, following up a knock of

150 with such fine bowling—he took 8 for 33—that he and
" E.M." (2 for 26) bowling unchanged, put their powerful
opponents out for 66, while in the follow-on the Doctor captured another 7 wickets for 46.   He was well supported by
his brothers in the field, " E.M." getting four catches and Fred
two.   Apart from the Graces, T. G. Matthews' 85 was the
only other notable feature of the Gloucestershire team.

There is unfortunately no record of the initial steps taken
by Dr. Henry Mills Grace to form the Gloucestershire Club;
the earliest minute book in the possession of the Club is for
1873, and a diligent search through the newspaper files for
1869 has revealed no account of a meeting having been held.
It is probable, however, that some time during 1869 or 1870
a meeting was held and that officers for a committee were
appointed.

Some years ago I had the good fortune to be presented by
M. Weeks, an old member of the Stapleton Cricket Club, with
a circular letter sent out by Dr. E. M. Grace in June, 1873, and
as this is one of the earliest documents issued by the county
club and gives the names of the officers and committee, I
reproduce it here in full: —

GLOUCESTERSHIRE COUNTY CRICKET CLUB
THORNBURY, Glos. R.S.O.

June, 1873

Dear Sir: —

The following matches are arranged to be played by the
county this season: —

June	9, 10, 11.	Gloucestershire v. Surrey, at the Oval.
	12, 13, 14.	Gloucestershire v. Sussex, at Brighton.
July	28, 29, 30.	Gloucestershire v. Yorkshire, at Sheffield.
August	14, 15, 16.	Gloucestershire v. Yorkshire, at Clifton.
	25, 26, 27.	Gloucestershire v. Surrey, at Clifton.
	28, 29, 30.	Gloucestershire v. Sussex, at Cheltenham.

These matches are necessarily a great expense to the county club   Will you, therefore, kindly become a subscriber to our funds?   The following are the committee for this season:—

PRESIDENT
His Grace the Duke of Beaufort, K.G., Badminton, Chippenham.

VICE-PRESIDENT
The Rt. Hon. Lord Fitzharding, Berkeley Castle, Gloucestershire.

TREASURER
William Henry Harford, Lawrence Weston, Henbury.

CAPTAIN
W. G. Grace, Downend, near Bristol.

SECRETARY
E. M. Grace, Thornbury, Gloucestershire.

COMMITTEE

Allen A. Bathhurst, M.P., Cirencester and 32, St. James's Place, London.
J. C. Bengough, The Ridge, Wootton-under-Edge.
J. Arthur Bush, 7, Rodney Place, Clifton.
Colonel Bush, Clifton.
S. H. Brookes, Cheltenham.
Rev. C. R. Davey, Tracy Park, near Bath.
Rev. Joseph Greene, Clifton.
Sir William V. Guise, Bt., Elmore Court, near Gloucester.
Henry Grace, Kingswood Hill, near Bristol.
William Henry Miles, Ham Green, near Bristol.
R. Fenton Miles, Clifton.
T. G. Matthews, Clifton.
Rev. C. H. Ridding, Slymbridge Vicarage, Nr. Stonehouse.
F. Townsend, Clifton.

Copy of Rule 6.   That an annual subscription of 10/- shall entitle a member to a ticket of admission to all matches played in the county, and a subscriber of £1 or upwards shall have a ticket to admit his family or a friend, if preferred, and a donation of £5. 5. 0. shall constitute a life member with the foregoing privileges.

We were very successful in 1872, only losing one match and that by only one wicket, and to keep the club in its present state of efficiency we require funds to bring forward any young players who are likely to become ornaments to the eleven. Therefore, I hope I may be allowed to place your name on the list of subscribers.

An early answer will much oblige.

Yours faithfully,

EDWARD   MILLS   GRACE,

Secretary to the Gloucestershire County Cricket Club.

It will be seen from the names included in this letter that the county was fortunate in receiving influential support, and it may be taken for granted that in the main the list figures in the original selection of officers to govern the club. Gloucestershire County Cricket history may be said to have started in 1870, when in addition to the games played against Surrey and the M.C.C. already mentioned, two matches were played with Glamorganshire who, of course, at that time did not rank as first-class. In view of the many disastrous visits of Gloucestershire to the Oval in later years, it must afford some consolation that they overwhelmed Surrey on their first visit to the ground : this ignominious defeat must have been a severe blow to the pride of Surrey—a county which for years had been almost invincible and was strong enough to have regular matches with An England XI. R. Fenton Miles, whose bowling had much to do with Surrey's downfall, was the first bowler to exploit the "off-theory," and coming down to Bristol from Clifton on the same bus as the veteran player some years ago (he was then over 80), he told me how it came about. He was bowling in one of the early games when " W.G." changed the position of the field and stationed a man at what afterwards became known as " extra cover." Then, as Mr. Miles was about to bowl, the Doctor whispered " Pitch one up a little wide on the off " and, this advice being followed, a catch by " extra cover " was the immediate result. R. F. Miles became, as is well known, a great bowler for Gloucestershire and many of his wickets came from pitching 'em up a little wide on the off. Other slow bowlers followed his example and so " off-theory," as it is called, became a general part of the attack, producing many victims until batsmen became wary and refused to be tempted.

In looking through the county club minute books some exceedingly interesting facts have been disclosed dealing with Gloucestershire's early history. The records are all in the familiar handwriting of Dr. E. M. Grace, who was Secretary to the club for no less a period than 39 years, from 1870 to 1909; they are brief but very little that is material is missed for "the little doctor," as he was often called, had a wonderful gift of recognising essential points whether it was at an inquest or a long drawn out committee meeting. The first meeting recorded in this first book of minutes, which covered a period of 15 years, was held at the White Lion Hotel, Bristol, on Thursday, March 20th, 1873, and there is an entry which records that " Nottinghamshire have retired from the Championship Cup matches at Lord's, Gloucestershire do the same but have matches with Yorkshire instead."

It will no doubt be news to present-day cricketers that in 1873 the M.C.C. decided to provide a challenge cup for competition by the counties, the object being to increase interest in county matches which at that time was at rather a low ebb. The expenses were to be borne by the M.C.C. and the cup was to be retained in perpetuity by the team which won the final tie in three successive years. The scheme looked a good one but it soon collapsed and actually only one match—Kent v. Sussex—was played, for by the rules of the contest each round had to be played at Lord's and the pitch there being in such bad condition (there were many injuries sustained in the Kent and Sussex match) that the other teams refused to play and that was the end of the Challenge Cup Competition.

It was at this first meeting of the county club in 1873 that the long series of colts matches in one of which—sixteen years later—I had the privilege of playing, was inaugurated. The first of these games took place at Gloucester and produced a recruit for the county team—Jack Painter—who rendered the club such splendid service as a professional. H. J. Broughton a great Rugby football player for Gloucester and afterwards President of the Gloucestershire Rugby Union, also played in

this match which, by the way, resulted in a defeat for the
county XI despite the presence of the three Graces ("E.M.,"
" W.G." and " G.F.") who took all twenty (one man was
absent) of the wickets which fell in the Colts' first innings and
fifteen in the second.

A squabble with Notts over the date of a fixture obtains
rather lengthy reference in the minutes of the next meeting
of the committee, and the secretary is instructed to write
to the Editor of " Bells' Life," and inform him that the committee had taken steps to arrange the differences between the
two counties and to express the hope that the public " will for
the present withhold their judgment on the whole affair." In
this matter W. G. Grace was involved and, at a subsequent
meeting, the committee felt it necessary to pass a resolution
exonerating him from all blame. Evidently the proceedings
of the committee were not always harmonious for, before the
quarrel with Notts was settled, the secretary found it necessary
to put in his minutes: —

> "After more conversation of not too polite a nature, as
> the Rev. J. Greene disputed the correctness of the notes
> taken by the secretary at the Committee meeting of the
> 20th, saying that his memory was superior to the black
> and white testimony of the secretary . . ."

This paragraph was obviously subject to criticism at a later
date and one imagines, by the difference in the ink used, that
it was crossed out by the chairman.

The minutes of the November meeting are so much to the
point that here they are in full: —

> " Committee meeting held at the White Lion Hotel,
> Bristol, on Thursday, November 25th, at 3 o'clock.
> Present: E. M. Grace, and that's all."

How characteristic of " E.M." this entry is; one would like to
know why no other member of the committee turned up. Pos-
sibly the " conversation " at the previous meeting referred to
by the secretary as " not too polite " had something to do with
the absence of those committeemen—Colonel Bush, T. G.
Matthews, F. Townsend, J. A. Bush and the Rev. J. Greene,
who had been fairly regular in their attendance throughout
1873.

ASHLEY GRANGE, BRISTOL

Where W. G. Grace lived for many years.

It is interesting to note that the first meeting in 1874 took place at the Grand Hotel, the name by which the White Lion was to be known in future and where, by the way, the County Club meetings continued to be held until 1935 when the meeting and dinner took place at the Royal Hotel. A variety of interesting items are noted in the minutes of this year. The committee fixed the scale for personal expenses for the players and it was also resolved that " in special cases application may be made by players for loss of time or out-of-pocket expenses, which shall invariably be submitted to the committee for their consideration, who shall be empowered to appropriate a reasonable sum to meet each particular case as it may come before them." Other entries for 1874 included : —

" That bats be given to the best average bat and bowler at Clifton College. Carried unanimously."

" That there shall be no bands this season either at Clifton or Cheltenham. Lost by one vote."

" That a bat be presented to the batsman making 50 runs in an innings for the county. Carried by one vote."

" That James Lillywhite shall have the management of the Cheltenham match and that he shall be paid Ten Pounds for so doing. Carried unanimously."

So much has been said and written about the financial aspect of the Graces' association with Gloucestershire cricket that the following entry in the minutes for October 22nd, 1874, should settle once and for all this much debated subject. The entry reads : —

"That Mr. W. G. Grace be paid £45 and Mr. G. F. Grace £35 for their expenses incurred while playing for the county in the year 1874."

It may also be added that the minutes also showed that Dr. E. M. Grace received for many years the sum of £60 for his services as secretary of the Club, a figure which by no stretch of imagination can be regarded as excessive, considering the amount of organising as well as clerical work involved.

In the minutes for 1874 there is also a reference to the catering at the matches on the Clifton College Ground and among those who were invited to tender for the privilege of supplying the refreshments was Mr. J. Gigg, who was for

many years connected with the catering department at the
Zoological Gardens, Clifton.

The annual meeting of 1875 was held on May 4th, with Mr.
J. Austin Ware in the chair, and the secretary in recording the
minutes states: —

> " Again there were very few members present, showing
> how little interest subscribers take in county cricket in
> Gloucestershire, or perhaps it is that they place such
> implicit confidence in their committee."

The names of those who attended are given; they number
seven! It is recorded that James Lillywhite attended the
meeting in 1877 in order to induce the committee to organise
a week's cricket at Cheltenham, but it was found to be impossible to make arrangements for that season. It was, however,
resolved to seek the consent of the Council of Cheltenham
College for a week's cricket annually during the vacation and,
this consent having been granted, the Cheltenham Festival was
inaugurated in 1878. The following year there is an entry in
the minutes of one of the meetings " That Mr. Lillywhite be
informed that he must give £150 and pay all local expenses for
the week's cricket at Cheltenham. If Mr. Lillywhite will not
give this sum, the Committee will manage the matches themselves."

Certain incidents prove that Dr. E. M. Grace was not, as is
generally supposed, allowed to rule the roost and trouble
arose at one meeting through him claiming, as a member, to
vote at committee meetings. The Rev. J. Greene, who often
presided, disputed this right and resigned and, on the matter
cropping up again, nine more members of the committee
resigned, including four members of the team—R. F. Miles,
J. A. Bush, F. Townsend and T. G. Matthews.

A terse entry by the secretary indicates that their resignation was accepted but at the next meeting they were re-elected,
" E.M." having intimated his intention of not exercising his
right to vote.

One notes with interest the election of members who for
many years afterwards rendered great service to the club. Mr.
J. W. Arrowsmith, who joined the committee in 1876, was
probably more concerned than anyone with the founding of
the County Ground at Ashley Down: Mr. H. W. Beloe, elected

in 1876, was for a long period chairman of the club. Familiar names occur in the list of subscribers recorded as attending the annual meetings: —

Arthur Robinson, Gerald Moseley, Charles Strachan, James Chard, F. N. Tribe, E. G. Clarke, E. W. Ball, T. Pakeman, Frank Wills and Wilberforce Tribe,

all of whom will be remembered as good citizens and sportsmen.

CHAPTER VIII

The season of 1871 provided " W.G." with a succession of wonderful innings and he scored no fewer than ten centuries, only one, however (116 v. Notts), being made for Gloucestershire.   His biggest score was 268 for the South against the North in H. H. Stephenson's Benefit Match at the Oval, incidentally the biggest score then made on that ground and a record which stood for some years. It was also the Champion's best effort to date and, being amassed in the second innings, fully compensated for his being bowled first ball by J. C. Shaw at his first attempt. In recognition of his fine batting " W.G." received not only a bat with a gold plate recording his feat from the Surrey Club but also a ring from H. H. Stephenson himself, who was delighted at his friend's success.

His second highest score that year, 217, was also made in a benefit match for the Gentlemen against the Players in John Lillywhite's testimonial game on Prince's Ground, Brighton; the coincidence did not end here either for, as in the previous match, his success came in the second innings following another failure against J. C. Shaw, who yet again bowled him for a " duck."   In scoring his second double century, " W.G." and his brother Fred put on 241 runs together before the latter was out for a brilliant 98, an entirely faultless innings and, at the conclusion of the match, both brothers received bats to mark their fine performances.

Although the Champion scored but one hundred for the county, Gloucestershire playing five matches won three of them and were only beaten once.   In the game against Surrey at the Oval, which they won by an innings, it says much for the batting strength of the Western county that a total of 315 was reached despite the fact that W. G. and E. M. Grace were dismissed for 1 and 3 respectively; Fred, however, made 69 and received valuable help from C. S. Gordon with 68 and R. F. Miles, who scored 79.   Surrey's second innings is notable for the fact that with but one exception all the wickets fell to a combination of the Grace family, and I herewith append the score-sheet of this innings:

SURREY, 2nd Innings

JUPP, c E. M. Grace, b W. G. Grace	45
R. HUMPHREY, b E. M. Grace	8
C. W. POTTER, c G. F. Grace, b E. M. Grace	5
POOLEY, b E. M. Grace	9
J. GREGORY, b W. G. Grace	10
T. HUMPHREY, not out	0
STEPHENSON, c and b E. M. Grace	1
GRIFFITH, c Strachen, b W. G. Grace	7
CLIFFORD, c E. M. Grace, b W. G. Grace	2
STREET, c E. M. Grace, b W. G. Grace	0
MARTIN, c G. F. Grace, b E. M. Grace	1
Extras	6
	94

" E.M." was the most successful bowler, taking 6 for 36, while " W.G.'s " four wickets cost only 17 runs.

The return game with Surrey at Clifton was rendered memorable by the magnificent batting of T. G. Matthews who, scoring 201, registered the first double century for the county; it was a fine innings and naturally overshadowed Fred Grace's 89, which was nevertheless an excellent knock.

During this summer " W.G." showed a partiality for the Notts bowling, scoring 78 and 55 off it in the drawn game at Clifton, and 79 and 116 at Trent Bridge; in the latter game, however, he was the only Gloucestershire batsman to face the bowling of J. C. Shaw with any confidence, and the home team won easily by 10 wickets.

" W.G.'s " record for 1871 was the excellent one of 2,390 runs, a total which far surpassed the achievements of any of his contemporaries and which sent his average up from 54.26 to 78.9—a truly great performance. The next best amateur bat in England that year was none other than the Doctor's young brother Fred, who averaged 37.16 runs per innings. This family success must have been a source of great joy to both Dr. and Mrs. H. M. Grace, but unhappily it was to be short-lived for two days after Christmas, 1871, Dr. Grace passed away at the comparatively early age of 63. The loss of their father must have been a sad blow to the brotherhood and not only to the Grace family but to all cricket enthusiasts in the county, who owed a great debt to Dr. Henry Mills Grace for his

untiring efforts in establishing the County Cricket Club. Dr.
Grace was a very keen churchman, deeply interested in every-
thing pertaining to the church, regularly attending parish
meetings and rendering every possible help in other directions.
One can easily believe that such a man was, as his tombstone
in the quaint country churchyard at Downend records, beloved,
respected and his passing was deeply regretted by all classes
in the county.

Increasing their programme in 1872 to 7 matches (they
played Surrey, Notts and Sussex twice and Yorkshire once),
Gloucestershire again suffered only one defeat and that by a
single wicket in the opening match with Surrey at the Oval. In
the return game against the Metropolitan county at Cheltenham, however, they took ample revenge, winning by an innings
thanks to the bowling of " W.G." who took in all 12 wickets
for 73 runs. Sussex were beaten at Clifton despite the fact that
the Champion was not playing and also that there was a first
innings deficit of 101. In this game it was Fred Grace who
came to the rescue with a fine bowling performance—he took
7 wickets for 43, and also made 44 runs. " E.M." also batted
very well for 41 and 32.

Outside county cricket the Champion again flogged the
Players' bowling to the tune of 117 at the Oval and 112 at
Lord's, while on the same ground he also scored a century for
the M.C.C. against Yorkshire.

At the close of the 1872 season, " W.G." visited Canada and
the United States as a member of R. A. FitzGerald's Amateur
team, which included the brothers E. and A. Lubbock, A. N.
(" Monkey ") Hornby, the Hon. G. Harris (afterwards the
great Lord Harris), A. Appleby of Lancashire, W. H. Hadow,
C. J. Ottaway, C. K. Francis, F. Pickering and W. M. Rose.
In his first innings of the tour against Montreal " W.G." made
81, an innings which was described by the local press as
follows:

> " Mr. Grace is a large framed, loose jointed man, and
> you would say that his gait is a trifle awkward and sham-
> bling, but when he goes into the field you see that he is
> quick sighted, sure-handed, and light-footed as the rest.
> He always goes in first and to see him tap the ball gently
> to the off for one, draw it to the on for two, pound it to

the limits for four, drive it beyond the most distant long leg for six, looks as easy as falling off a log."

He made his initial century in Canada against Toronto, scoring 142 and as a result of this innings was offered two bears to take back to England with him; needless to say he did not accept this queer offer.

1873 was indeed a proud year for Gloucestershire cricket for at the end of the season they found themselves Champions among the first-class cricketing counties, winning four games out of six and not being beaten once. Of course, in these days of long fixture lists it does not seem quite fair that Gloucestershire, who played only six games, should take precedence over Yorkshire who, playing 13 matches, won 7 and lost 5. The brothers Grace contributed greatly to the county's victory over Surrey at the Oval for after " E.M." and " G.F." had put their opponents out for 131, Gilbert and Edward scoring 83 and 70 respectively, helped Gloucestershire to a match-winning total of 290. In Surrey's second innings, " E.M." and Fred again bowled well, their final figures for the match being " E.M." 6 for 139, and " G.F." 12 for 137.

At Brighton where the Western county won by the narrow margin of 9 runs, " E.M." with 76 in the second innings accomplished the best batting performance, while Gilbert took 6 wickets for 70, and Fred 9 for 83. Beating Yorkshire twice, " W.G." made 79 at Sheffield, while at Clifton Fred carried his bat for 165, a grand innings which somewhat overshadowed " E.M.'s " modest effort of 64.

Outside county games Gilbert scored six hundreds, his best score being 192 not out for the South against the North, while as usual he took centuries off the Players both at Lord's and the Oval, and 70 in the match at Prince's. His average of 79 for the season was his best to date and at the close of the summer he accepted the Marylebone's Club invitation to take a team to Australia in the coming winter.

On October 9th, 1873, one of the greatest events in the life of the Champion took place; he was married. The wedding was solemnised at St. Matthias' Church, South Kensington, and the bride was Miss Agnes Nicholls Day, a sweet and gentle lady who was often seen at Gloucestershire matches and was just as keen on following the achievements of her

famous husband as was his mother. " W.G.'s " best man was
his old friend, J. Arthur Bush, the Gloucestershire wicket-
keeper, and here is a notice of the wedding which appeared in
the local papers : —

> GRACE-DAY, October 9th, 1873. At the church of St.
> Matthias, West Brompton, by the Rev. John Dann, M.A.,
> brother-in-law of the bridegroom, assisted by the Rev.
> C. S. Haines, M.A., Vicar, and the Rev. A. J. K. Mac-
> Donald, William Gilbert Grace, fourth son of the late
> Henry Mills Grace, M.R.C.S. (Lond.) of Downend,
> Gloucestershire, to Agnes Nicholls Day, daughter of
> William Day of 19, Colehean Road, S.W.

Very soon after the wedding the bride and bridegroom left
with the English cricketers for Australia and included in the
party were Arthur Bush, the best man, and Gilbert's young
brother Fred. All the matches of his tour were played against
odds of 15, 18 or 22, and the final record of 10 wins, 3 losses
and 2 drawn games was highly creditable. The Champion,
as captain of the English team, lived up to his great reputation,
for he headed the batting with an average of 39 for 23 innings
and captured 65 wickets at the small cost of 7.42 runs apiece.
One gathers in looking up the records of this tour that things
did not pass off without disturbing incidents. In the controversy over Midwinter, the Australian player who afterwards
played for Gloucestershire as a professional, " W.G." hints at
trouble with Mr. Conway while in Australia, and a report in
one of the Australian papers stated : —

> " Now it may be confessed, if only in a shamefaced
> fashion that in Australia we did not take kindly to
> " W.G." For so big a man he is surprisingly tenacious
> on very small points. We duly admired him at the wicket,
> but thought him too apt to wrangle in the spirit of a
> duo-decimo attorney over small points of the game."

A cricket tour in Australia 75 years ago was vastly different
from what it is to-day; most of the travelling was done by
coach and on one of these journeys the cricketers were lost in
the bush. At one place—Stawell—the field on which the
match was to be played had been ploughed up three months
before and sown with grass so that a nice new pitch should be
ready when the English team arrived. Unfortunately it proved

to be so "nice" that the visitors were bundled out for 43 in just over an hour and suffered a heavy defeat.

The umpiring apparently was not the least of the troubles with which the tourists had to contend and, on one occasion, an Australian batsman who was clearly stumped was given "not out." On being asked to explain his decision, the umpire replied that Mr. Bush had had the tip of his nose in front of the wicket.

"W.G." has recorded too that in one game there was so much dust on the pitch that the ball sometimes stopped where it was pitched by the bowler, while at another town a bushel of stones had to be swept off the pitch before the game could be started. An interesting fact in connection with this, the third visit of an English team to Australia, was that for the first time the telegraph was used to acquaint people of the results.

On his return from Australia in 1874, "W.G." lost no time in showing that the trip had had no ill-effects on him for he opened the season by helping Gloucestershire to an innings victory over Sussex at Brighton, by scoring 179 and taking 11 wickets for 14 runs each. Keeping up this fine all-round form, he contributed largely to another big win, this time over Yorkshire at Sheffield, by amassing 167 runs and then capturing 12 wickets for 104. In the return game at Clifton, he once again punished the Yorkshire bowlers, hitting up 127, and following it up with another splendid bowling performance— 12 wickets at just over 10 runs each. Both "E.M." and Fred also batted well in this game, scoring 51 and 81 respectively. As a bowler "W.G.'s" biggest success was in 1874, his 14 wickets for 66 against Surrey at Cheltenham, when he and Fred, bowling unchanged, dismissed their opponents for a meagre 27 in their first innings; the Champion's analysis reading 7 for 18, while Fred's showed 3 for 8. Gloucestershire gained 4 wins—all by an innings—out of 6 games, their only defeat being a surprise one by Surrey in the opening game at the Oval. In all first-class cricket in 1874, "W.G." scored 8 centuries, but only one reached three figures for the Gentlemen, at Prince's: at Lord's incidentally, the Players managed to win for once in a way. At the end of the season the Champion had scored over 2,000 runs for Gloucestershire in county matches with an average of 66, the nearest other county player to him being his own brother Fred, who totalled 1,199

runs at 35 per innings. " E.M.'s " aggregate for the first
five seasons was just over 800 with an average of 26. From
these figures it will be seen what a tower of strength the
brothers Grace were to Gloucestershire for only two other
players—Frank Townsend and T. G. Matthews—scored over
500 runs for the county between 1870 and 1874.

1875 was a season of soft and sticky wickets; " W.G." described it as pre-eminently a bowler's year and in consequence
there were few outstanding batting performances for Gloucestershire. Undoubtedly the best innings played for the county
that summer was Fred Grace's 180 not out against Surrey at
Clifton, an excellent effort which, coupled with the fine
bowling of " W.G."—6 for 70—in the first innings, and that
of " E.M."—7 for 46—in the second, enabled Gloucestershire
to win easily by an innings. The Champion could only muster
three centuries during the season—two for the county—but
he once again took toll of the Players' attack at Lord's and was
not dismissed until he had run up a score of 152. At the
Oval for the Gentlemen against the Players, another member
of the Gloucestershire XI distinguished himself—G. Strachan
—who afterwards became captain of Surrey, accomplishing a
fine piece of bowling by taking the last 5 wickets in just over
8 overs for no runs.

As a bowler in 1875, "W.G." enjoyed a most successful
season, capturing 192 wickets for 12 runs each—the best season of his career with the ball.

Lord Hawke has placed on record his opinion that " W.G."
seemed to love the Yorkshire bowling and you have only to
look up the scores of the matches between the two counties
during the '70s to see that his Lordship had good reason for
making this statement. In fact, so remarkable were the
Champion's figures against Yorkshire during this period that
I make no excuse for giving his record from 1872 to 1877.

1872.	For M.C.C. at Lord's	101 and 43 not out.
	For Gloucestershire at Sheffield	150
1873.	For Gloucestershire at Sheffield	79 and 15 not out.
	at Clifton	21 and 25.
1874.	For Gloucestershire at Sheffield	167.
	at Clifton	127..

1875. For Gloucestershire at Sheffield 111 and 43.
at Clifton 37 and 17.
1876. For Gloucestershire at Sheffield 19 and 57.
at Cheltenham 318 not out.
1877. For Gloucestershire at Sheffield 9 and 84.
at Clifton 71.

Thus in 19 innings (3 times not out), " W.G." scored 1,494 runs off the Yorkshire bowlers for the amazing average of 93.33 runs per innings, proof indeed of his partiality for the Tykes' attack. In addition to the scores given, he also made 170 for England against a Combined Yorkshire and Notts XI in 1872. The array of bowling talent available on this occasion was exceptional, including as it did the great Alfred Shaw, then at his best, and Richard Iddison, a famous lob bowler, both of whom bowled slow stuff; then came Tom Emmett, Allan Hill and J. C. Shaw, probably the three best fast bowlers of that period. Hill was the terror of most batsmen and few bowlers have been more successful at hitting the stumps, his complete record for Yorkshire being 499 wickets of which no fewer than 341 were clean bowled. In this game, however, as in many others when he had to bowl to the Champion, Hill met his master in W. G. Grace and even he could not prevent the Doctor from adding yet another hundred to his growing list of three-figure innings. An interesting fact about this game was that play was prolonged to a later hour than any other important fixture in which " W.G." took part, stumps not being drawn until close on 8 o'clock. There was, however, an occasion when the Doctor was touring Canada with R. A. FitzGerald's team where a match was finished in almost total darkness.

A tribute to the Champion's wonderful physique is paid by the late Richard Daft, " W.G.'s " nearest rival for many years, who said: " His astounding feats could have been accomplished by no other man, however good a player, who was not possessed of great physical advantage, an iron constitution, and who did not live temperately." You have only to study " W.G.'s " bowling record at this period of his career to be impressed by the truth of Daft's judgment. The Doctor must have loved bowling to Yorkshire almost as much as he did batting against them, for during the period from 1872—1877 he captured no less than 84 of their wickets at the cost of about of 12 runs each.

It is not easy at this distance of time to realise how completely this black-bearded giant dominated the cricket fields of England. " PUNCH " found in the devastating form of this man from the West Country a never failing source of inspiration for cartoon and verse, and even the heavy-handed leader writers of the day dropped Gladstone and Disraeli and wrote about the nearest rival they had in the popular imagination. In one of these editorial discourses was written : —

" So deep is the apprehension entertained by every cricketer who is liable to find himself in one or another match ranged on the side to which Mr. Grace does not belong that grave propositions have been made in the higher councils of the craft, having for their purpose the memorialising of that gentleman, in terms of earnest supplication, entreating that he will consent to play for the future either blindfolded or with his right arm tied behind his back. Only by such a reduction of his extraordinary physical resources can the memorialists hope to dub him down to the level of ordinary good cricketers."

Another popular periodical came out in 1873 with the following suggestions : —

" That W. G. Grace shall owe a couple of hundreds or so before batting — these to be reckoned against the side should he not wipe them off.

" That his shoe spikes should be turned inwards.

" That he shall be declared ' out ' whenever the umpire likes.

" That he shall always be the eleventh player.

" That he shall not be allowed to play at all."

From all this it is easy to see what a figure of national importance he had become in the eyes of both Press and Public alike.

CHAPTER IX

Great as had been " W.G.'s " batting triumphs before 1876, those accomplished during that year surpassed all his former achievements. Twice during this season he broke his own personal record with innings of over 300, scoring 344 for the M.C.C. against Kent at Canterbury, and 318 not out for Gloucestershire against Yorkshire at Cheltenham. Thanks to his amazing batting during August the county was able to return to its former position at the top of the Championship, winning five matches out of eight, and going through the season unbeaten. " W.G.," strange to relate, did not open at all promisingly with the bat, being out for 1 against Surrey at the Oval, but redeemed this failure by taking 8 wickets in the game for 132; while in the return match at Clifton he bowled even better, capturing 6 wickets in the first innings for 35. It was at Brighton against Sussex that he started to "lay on the wood," a fine second innings of 104 enabling Gloucestershire to win after being behind on the first innings. A narrow win of 17 runs over Yorkshire at Sheffield was due almost entirely to the all-round performances of " W.G." and Fred, who scored 57 and 42 respectively, and took all the Yorkshire wickets between them in the first innings for 79 runs.

Then came that great week in August when in three innings the Champion totalled 839 runs:

344 for M.C.C. v. Kent at Canterbury
177 for Gloucestershire v. Notts at Clifton
and 318 not out for Gloucestershire v. Yorks. at Cheltenham.

Against any sort of bowling this scoring would have been considered phenomenal, but in each of these games " W.G.," who was now 28, had to bat against men who were among the best bowlers of the day. Kent, for instance, had G. G. Hearne, W. Foord-Kelsey and C. A. Absolom; Notts, Alfred Shaw and Morley, while Yorkshire's attack included Allan Hill, Ulyett, Tom Emmett and T. Armitage, the last named being a notable lob bowler who shares with W. Humphreys of Sussex

and R. C. Tinley of Notts the distinction of being the best
exponents of underarm deliveries, and was chosen to tour
Australia with Jas. Lillywhite's team the same year. The day-
to-day progress towards this huge total of 839 runs is so
uncommon that it is set down so far as I know, for the first
time:

Friday	133 runs
Saturday	211 runs
Monday	177 runs
Tuesday	did not bat
Wednesday	did not bat
Thursday	216 runs
Friday	102 runs

It took "W.G." $17\frac{1}{2}$ hours to score the runs, and his hits
included 2 sevens, 4 sixes, 4 fives and 103 fours. It is a matter
of cricket history, too, that during the 17 hours in which he
was meeting the best bowling that Kent, Notts and Yorkshire
could produce, he gave only two chances. At Canterbury, all
the Kent XI, except the wicket-keeper, bowled; seven of the
eleven Notts players tried to dislodge him at Clifton, while at
Cheltenham the fielders were so demoralised after eight
bowlers had done their best that the Captain, Ephraim Lockwood, did not find it at all easy to persuade anyone to bowl.
In fact, it is related that Hill having declined to take on at one
end, Emmett shouted to Lockwood, " Why don't you make
him bowl, you're Captain!" To which Hill replied, " Why don't
you bowl yourself? You're frightened!" This reply stung
Emmett, who had already bowled over 50 overs, so much that
he took the ball and sent down three wides in succession.
Gloucestershire totalled 528, to which Yorkshire replied with
127 for 7 before the match was given up as a draw.

The match against Notts at Clifton College on August 14th,
1876, has always interested me because it was my first experience of county cricket. Memories of the occasion, however,
are rather dim. Had I been old enough I would undoubtedly
have joined in the shout which went up when "W.G." hit
a ball from Oscroft clean out of the ground, and also for
another hit for which seven were run. Of these incidents, however, my memory is unresponsive but a detailed report of the
game before me indicates that the three Graces—"W.G.,"
" E.M." and " G.F."—totalled no fewer than 304 of the 419

runs which Gloucestershire scored from the bat, while the Champion completed his triumph by taking eight of the Notts wickets in the second innings for 69, thus enabling the home county to win by 10 wickets. Fred, with 98 for once out and 6 wickets for 80, also enjoyed a good match.

Judged solely from a point of physical endurance this wonderful week's cricket was an accomplishment which has never been equalled. The boundary system not yet having been generally adopted, it was still the custom at Clifton College to run out every hit unless the ball was sent out of the ground, and " W.G.'s " square leg hit for 7 was at the top end of the ground by the Chapel. Many years after I saw Curtis, one of the best bats the College has ever produced, make a hit for which, I believe, 9 were run. The mileage represented by those 839 runs is, of course, impossible to state but it must have been considerable and there was also the wear and tear of bowling and fielding " W.G." must have been proof in those days against reaction from excessive physical strain, and the other brothers were much the same; it is, however, a significant fact that not one of the five brothers lived to be an old man.

In scoring his 344 against Kent. " W.G." broke not only his personal record but also that of Mr. Ward who, in 1820, scored 278 for the M.C.C. against Norfolk at Lord's, an innings which remained the record for first-class cricket for 56 years, and the record for the ground until 1925 when Percy Holmes of Yorkshire surpassed it with 315 not out against Middlesex.

As usual, " W.G.'s " series of big scores were received with an outburst of eulogy in rhyme, of which the following is a typical example : —

> " Pavilions thunder the well-earned applause
>   " While still he keeps gallantly on,
> " Repeating his scoring of threes and fours
>   " Till all his companions are gone.
> " Triumphantly then he crosses the ground,
>   " NOT OUT with three hundred is he,
> " Eclipsing the once famous doings of Ward
>   " The Invincible " W.G."!"

During 1876, " W.G." not only scored more than double the
number of runs of his nearest rival, Lockwood, but was also
second to Alfred Shaw in the total of wickets taken, a performance which marked the peak of his all-round achievements.
From 1868 to 1880 he was so much the leader of English batsmen that only in two seasons—1875 and 1878-- did he fail to
top the averages.

Among the outstanding events in Gloucestershire cricket in
the 70's was the inauguration of the Cheltenham Cricket Week
by James Lillywhite, a member of a famous Sussex cricketing
family and a most interesting personality, who, having settled
in Cheltenham in 1855 as coach to the College, was active in
a variety of directions promoting the interests of the game.
Cheltenham's first experience of county cricket was in 1872, the
arrangements, as has already been recorded, being entrusted to
Lillywhite who received an honorarium of £10 for his services.
According to a " Brief History of the Cheltenham Week,"
published in 1906, the proposal for the festival took definite
shape during a convivial evening at the " Plough Hotel " after
the Notts match in 1877. The Minutes of the County Club
Committee show, however, that Lillywhite interviewed the
members at the Grand Hotel, Bristol, some months before this
and tried, unsuccessfully, to persuade them to allot two games
to Cheltenham during 1877, an innovation which took place
the following year. Apparently, Lillywhite took full respon-
sibility for the two matches and had to stand the risk of bad
weather for the Minutes of a meeting record that ". . . Jas.
Lillywhite offered £140 for the week's cricket at Cheltenham,
as last year, but asked that if wet, or not a success, £10 should
be given back to him." Evidently the Committee were keen
business men for it was resolved " that he should give £140,
wet or dry, success or no success." The veteran cricketer, alas,
did not live to see the festival become the popular event it has
been for so many years. In October, 1882, he was seriously
ill, a fact which led to the following entry in the Minute
Book: " RESOLVED that in the event of the death of Jas.
Lillywhite before the matches at Cheltenham in 1883, his son-
in-law, Mr. Lawrence, or representatives of the family, shall
have the management of the Week, the same as he has hitherto
done." He died in November, and in accordance with the
resolution the Festival was managed in the following and subsequent years by his son-in-law, Mr. Edwin Lawrence, whom

the Committee made a Life Member of the Club in 1887, as a mark of appreciation for his services.

The Cheltenham College Close has provided most of us who have followed the fortunes of Gloucestershire cricket for any long period with pleasant memories, yet it is a curious fact that except for his innings of 318 not out, against Yorkshire in 1876, "W.G." achieved no outstanding batting performances on that ground during the '70's, when on other grounds he was in such wonderful form. The first Gloucestershire player to register a century at Cheltenham was Frank Townsend who, in 1873, made 136 against Sussex; twenty-six years later his son, Charles L. Townsend, played a magnificent knock of 135 against the Australians, an innings that ranks as one of the best ever played on that ground.

Most great cricketers have in the course of their careers struck a ground where, for some inexplicable reason, they have found a spell cast over them. "W.G.'s" unlucky ground was most surely the Cheltenham College ground, for although he did not miss a county game there from 1872 to 1898, he only exceeded the hundred on five occasions, indeed in 77 innings there his scores of more than 50 number only 14, but on the other hand he was only out for a "Duck" four times. "W.G." may have disappointed the Cheltenham crowd with his batting but he achieved some splendid bowling feats there. Here are some of them:

1872	v.	Surrey	12	for	73
1873	v.	Sussex	8	for	37
1874	v.	Surrey	14	for	66
1877	v.	Notts	17	for	89
1878	v.	Sussex	13	for	103
1878	v.	Yorkshire	8	for	87
1879	v.	Yorkshire	5	for	68

E. M. Grace, who played at Cheltenham for 21 years, never made a century there, and strange to say G. L. Jessop scored only one.

One of the happiest moments in "W.G.'s" life must have been on July 23rd, 1879, when he received a national testimonial consisting of a cheque for £1,458, a marble clock, and two bronze ornaments, the presentation being made, most fit-

tingly, in front of the pavilion at Lord's. A match, Over 30 v.
Under 30, had just been concluded, and it had been arranged as
a complimentary game in " W.G.'s " honour, the proceeds going
to swell the testimonial fund, but whatever the amount was the
Doctor never touched a penny of it. Earlier in the year the
benefit match of his old friend, Alfred Shaw, had been ruined
by bad weather, so " W.G.," being among the many who
sympathised with the Notts professional, took the unprecedented step of writing to the M.C.C. requesting that the whole
of the proceeds of his own complimentary match should be
handed over to Shaw. This request was granted and Shaw's
subscription list benefited by a substantial amount. This
generous action was in keeping with the Champion's practical
consideration for his professional comrades throughout his
long cricketing career. He would not, if he could help
it, allow anything to interefere with his playing in a
benefit match, and the Minute Book of the Gloucestershire Club shows the determined stand he made to have
the date of a county match altered so that he might play in old
Luke Greenwood's benefit at Sheffield. When Edgar Willsher's
testimonial was spoiled by rain, it was " W.G." who arranged
another game—his own XI v. Kent—which proved a great
success. No wonder that the Grand Old Man was beloved by
the professionals, and his thoughtfulness in this direction was
proved long after he had left Gloucestershire by his coming
down from London to take part in John Spry's benefit on the
County Ground, Bristol.

1877 saw Gloucestershire retain the championship with
" W.G." claiming the highest aggregate, 1,474, for the season.
Strangely enough he scored only two centuries—261 for the
South v. the North at Prince's, and 110 for Combined Gloucestershire and Yorkshire XI v. England at Lord's. Although the
Doctor failed to reach three figures for the county, Gloucestershire improved even on their previous good record, winning 7
matches out of 8, .and remaining unbeaten. Opening the season
with a match against England at the Oval, the western county
proved victorious by five wickets, the honours in a low scoring
match going to Gloucestershire's first regular professional,
Midwinter, whom " W.G." had discovered in Australia (actually he was born in Gloucestershire) and who took 11 wickets
for 82. For his county, " W.G.'s " best batting efforts were
his 84 and 71, both against Yorkshire at Sheffield and Clifton,

respectively. "E.M." topped the county batting averages this year with an average of 29, while second and third came Fred and "W.G." Outside county matches, Fred with 134 scored his first century for the Gentlemen at the Oval.

The following year, which was notable for the visit of the first Australian team to this country, saw "W.G." score only one hundred, while Gloucestershire, who showed a decided falling off, failed to retain the title of Champions. It was during this season that one of the most singular of the many episodes in which the Doctor took part occurred; it concerned the "kidnapping" of Midwinter, the Australian professional. On June 20th Gloucestershire were due to meet Surrey at the Oval, while on the same day the Australians were playing Middlesex at Lord's. When play was about to commence at the Oval it was discovered that Gloucestershire were a man short; Midwinter had failed to turn up. Telling "E.M." to carry on, "W.G." left the ground, hailed a four-wheeler telling the cabby to drive to Lord's at fast as possible. Here "W.G.'s" suspicions were confirmed. There was Midwinter sitting with his pads on waiting to bat for the Australians. What the Doctor said to Midwinter will never be known, but it was not long before they were both outside the ground and in a cab on the way to the Oval, a journey that the Australian was likely to remember for the rest of his life. The sequel to this amazing incident is revealed in the County Committee's Minutes for July 1st, 1878, when the Secretary reported the receipt of a letter from the Australian manager demanding an apology from Mr. W. G. Grace, otherwise the two fixtures with Gloucestershire would be cancelled. The story from both sides is further revealed in copies of correspondence entered in the Minute Book: "W.G.'s" case was that Midwinter had arranged to play for Gloucestershire whenever required, while the Australians contended that he had promised to play for them and that when a deputation consisting of David Gregory, the captain, H. F. Boyle, and Mr. Conway, the manager, waited upon "W.G." for an explanation at the Oval, they were insulted. Naturally the Gloucestershire captain felt aggrieved, and to those who knew him it is not difficult to conjure up the scene when this deputation waited on him, and there can be no doubt that some very hard words were used. In fact, David Gregory quoted what the Doctor did say, and it was not at all complimentary but was justifiable for, according to "W.G.'s" version the Australians had caused Midwinter to break his engagement with the County by the promise of higher pay.   "W.G." strongly denied insulting the Australians as a body; his remarks, he said, being directed against Mr. Conway, the manager, with whom he had had previous trouble both here and in Australia. He was, however, if the other members of the deputation, Messrs. Gregory and Boyle, felt sore over his remarks, quite ready to apologise to them, but not to Mr. Conway. Unfortunately this was not enough for the Australians, who adhered to their original intention that they would scratch the two fixtures with Gloucestershire unless they received full and ample apology, and they even went so far as to reserve the right to publish such amende.   The Gloucestershire committee must have had a most worrying time over the whole affair, which was eventually settled and closed with the following entry in the minutes : —

" Mr. W. G. Grace wrote a letter of apology to the Australians," and a copy of a letter from the Australian captain saying they were quite satisfied.

This, by the way, was not the only bother that the first Australian team had during the tour, there was also a dispute over their match with the Players at the Oval, some of the leading professionals refusing to play because they were not satisfied with the terms offered them by the Tourists.

" W.G." took part in the now historic match between the M.C.C. and the Australians at Lord's on May 27th, when F. R. Spofforth and H. F. Boyle dismissed a strong XI which included as well as " W.G.," such good players as A. N. Hornby, A. J. Webbe, Flowers, G. G. Hearne, Jun., Alfred Shaw and Morley, for 33 and 19.   Although the Australians could only muster 41 runs in their first innings they won by 9 wickets.   The Doctor in company with the rest of the team failed, being dismissed for 4 and 0; in his second innings he was clean bowled by the " Demon " Spofforth.

Gloucestershire's two encounters with the Australians, both of which took place on the Clifton College ground, resulted in a win for the visitors in the first game, but in the second the county held them to a draw in which the home team led on the first innings.   In this game, " E.M." collected 55 runs, while Fred made 15, but " W.G." once again fell a victim to Spofforth who bowled him before he had opened his account;

as a bowler, however, he made amends, taking 4 wickets for 44.

Besides " W.G.," both " E.M." and Fred appeared for the Gentlemen of England against the Australians at Prince's, a game which resulted in an innings defeat for the Tourists thanks to the batting, in a low scoring match, of " W.G." and W. Gilbert who scored 25 and 20 respectively, and the fine bowling of A. G. Steel who captured 11 wickets for 72. " W.G." also bowled well, his analysis showing 6 wickets for 52 runs while " E.M." distinguished himself in the field by making three good catches.

At Lord's, for the Gentlemen, " W.G." scored 90 in the first innings, but after making 2 at his second attempt was clean bowled by Alfred Shaw, the ball being described as " one that would have beaten Old Nick himself." In the match at the Oval, the Doctor was first in and last out for 40 runs scored out of 76, an innings which was said to have been without a chance. Despite his efforts, the Players led on the first innings by 46, but thanks to another good innings by " W.G." of 63, and a contribution by Fred of 35, the Gentlemen were able to set the Professionals 157 to win, a task which proved beyond their powers by 55 runs. Of the Gentlemen, " W.G.'s " bowling figures of 3 for 20 were the best.

1879 was pronounced by expert cricketers to be the worst season ever known, and certainly, from early May to late August, there were scarcely three consecutive days of summer weather, which led in consequence to an unprecedented number of drawn games. Gloucestershire again fared only moderately and for the first time suffered a defeat at home, Notts winning at Cheltenham by six wickets despite the fact that " W.G." and Midwinter put them out for 65 in the first innings. The Doctor's figures in this game were 6 wickets for 37. In spite of the county's moderate displays, " W.G." continued to demonstrate his all-round ability, and headed both batting and bowling tables for Gloucestershire, his record being:

Batting—709 runs. Top score 123. Average 54.
Bowling—75 wickets at 12 runs apiece.

His batting average was far above that of Frank Townsend who was second with 23.

The Champion and Midwinter were fast proving themselves to be an excellent bowling combination, and here are some of their efforts in 1879: —

" W.G." 9—95, Midwinter 6—83 v. Surrey at the Oval.

" W.G." 15 for 116 v. Surrey at Clifton.

" W.G." 6 for 16, Midwinter 2 for 25 (1st innings) v. Middx. at Lord's.

" W.G." 7 for 37, Midwinter 3 for 12 (1st innings) v. Lanca-shire at Clifton.

" W.G." 6 for 37, Midwinter 4 for 23 (1st innings) v. Notts. at Cheltenham.

In his testimonial match at Lord's, " W.G.," with 0 and 7, did not shine as a batsman, but made up in no small way for this defect by his bowling, his record for the match being 9 wickets for 87 of which 6 fell to him for 32 runs in the second innings. " E.M.," who opened the " Over 30 " innings with " W.G.," scored 73 for once out while Fred, who was on the opposite side, carried his bat for 35 in the first innings.

Although reference has already been made to the presentation to " W.G.," it may be of interest if a more detailed account of those memorable proceedings are reproduced here:

" PRESENTATION TO MR. W. G. GRACE.

" The presentation to Mr. W. G. Grace took place yesterday at the most appropriate spot which could have been selected, viz., in front of the Pavilion at Lord's. It consisted of a sum of money, a marble clock, bearing the inscription ' PRESENTED TO W. G. GRACE ON JULY 23RD, 1879, ON THE OCCASION OF THE MATCH, OVER 30 v. UNDER 30, PLAYED AT LORD'S,' and a pair of bronze ornaments representing Egyptian obelisks.

" Lord Fitzharding, who had kindly undertaken to make the presentation, regretted his inability to control the weather, as he thought there were few such interesting occasions as that which had brought them together. Referring to the Testimonial, his Lordship said that the original idea had been to purchase a practice for Mr. Grace, but having talked it over with the Duke of Beaufort they had decided that Mr. Grace was old enough to take care of himself (laughter and cheers) and they would leave him to choose a practice for himself. The total amount, deducting expenses, which would be placed to Mr. Grace's credit, including the value of the clock and the two ornaments, was about £1,400. (Cheers.) He had, accordingly, great pleasure in presenting the Testimonial to Mr. Grace and could only say, on behalf of the people of Gloucestershire, that they wished him as much success in his profession as he had reaped on the cricket field. (Loud cheers.)

" Mr. Grace, after stating that he was not a speech-maker, made a short and appropriate reply, in which he thanked them all for the way in which they had organised the Testimonial. It had far exceeded expectations, and whenever he looked at the clock he would remember the occasion on which it was presented to him.

" Lord Charles Russell, who had been asked as the oldest member of the Marylebone Club to say a few words afterwards, said ' he was not satisfied with the amount. £1,400 was an odd sum to present to anyone, and he pledged his word that it would be £1,500 before they had done with it. He was an old cricketer, and the enjoyment he had had in the cricket-field for many years past was in seeing Mr. Grace play cricket. He looked upon cricket as the sport of the people, from Prince to peasant, and was delighted to see it increase in popularity year by year, and that in some respects it was being better played. He had seen better bowling than was seen now. He had seen better men in that department of the game than Mr. Grace, but he could say with a clear conscience that he had never seen a better field (cheers) and had never seen anyone approach him as a batsman. (Cheers.) The game must be played with the head and the heart, and in this respect Mr. Grace was eminently prominent. Looking at Mr. Grace's playing, he was never able to tell whether that gentleman was playing a winning or a losing game. He had never seen the slightest lukewarmness or inertness in him in the field. (Cheers.) If they wanted to see Mr. Grace play cricket, he would ask them to look at him playing one ball. They all know the miserably tame effect of the ball hitting the bat instead of the bat hitting the ball, whether acting on the offensive or the defensive. In playing a ball, Mr. Grace put every muscle into it from the sole of his foot to the crown of his head. (Laughter.) His heart and soul were in the game, and he (Lord Russell) had never heard a bell go to start play, but Mr. Grace was in the field first. The game was a game of laws and regulations; if they relaxed these then it became merely a pastime fit for young men with nothing else to do, or middle-aged men who wanted to get an appetite. (Laughter and cheers.) The Marylebone Club held its ground for the promotion and practice of good sound cricket, and it was for that reason they had such delight in taking part in this testimonial to Mr. Grace, who was in every way a thorough cricketer. (Loud cheers.) Allusion had been made to H.R.H. the Prince of Wales having joined the subscribers; it might be presumption to speculate on his Royal Highness's motives for doing so, but he might hazard that H.R.H. was grateful to Mr. Grace for affording him the opportunity of showing his respect for the one great game of the people, requiring in those who play it the national essentials of patience, fortitude and pluck, and fostering the respect for law and love of fair play which are characteristic of the English people. (Loud cheers.) ' "

I must apologise for having reproduced this description in full, but I feel it is necessary, if only to show how high in the esteem of all classes " W.G." stood as early in his career as 1879, when he was just 31 years of age.

CHAPTER X

I have been asked many times by young cricketers who never had the privilege of seeing the great " W.G." pass down the pavilion steps and out on to the ground to open a Gloucestershire innings, to describe what his batting was like; what were his special strokes, and what sort of bowling he liked best. This is a task I could never satisfactorily accomplish: nearly every cricketer of eminence has produced runs by some distinctive characteristic—quickness of footwork, adroitness of wrist play, or unwearied patience in waiting for the perfectly safe ball to hit. There was, however, nothing about " W.G.'s " batting that you could describe as distinctive, save that he managed somehow to get nearly every ball in the middle of the bat, and you could no more associate a lucky snick through the slips or to leg with his batting than you could visualise Mendelssohn writing jazz. He was such a master of batting craft that he made the compilation of a huge score a matter of course. With regard to bowling preference it is generally assumed by cricket historians that he was happier with the ball which came to him fast and straight and the faster the better, than when it was delivered slowly by an expert in length and spin, but if you follow his triumphal progress through the 70's you will find that his great scores were made against the best of all varieties of bowling. Against the greatest of all slow bowlers, Alfred Shaw, in Gentlemen v. Players matches and in county games, " W.G." played many three-figure innings, and later in the 80's and early 90's such famous bowlers as George Lohmann, of Surrey, and Johnny Briggs, of Lancashire, could only claim to have bowled him on seven occasions.

What a wonderful decade for Gloucestershire cricket was 1870-79, for during this period they played 78 matches with first-class counties including two against England, and two with the Australians, and could boast of the magnificent record of 39 Won, 25 Drawn, and only 14 Lost. This record would have delighted the heart of Dr. Henry Mills Grace, had he been spared to see the realisation of his ambitions and the fulfilment of his untiring labours, which had, without doubt, done much to put Gloucestershire on the map of first-class cricket.

During the 70's it was the three Graces, " E.M.," " W.G.," and " G.F.," who exercised such a dominating influence over Gloucester cricket, but actually it was Gilbert who, by his superb batting and, at times, unplayable bowling, paved the way to its success, and those who cannot understand any cricketer of a past generation being equal to the great players —there is no need to mention names—of recent years, should study cricket history and especially the history of the 70's and the conditions under which the first half of the Champion's centuries were made.   There was an innings of his at Lord's in 1870—M.C.C. v. Yorkshire—which was regarded at the time as a miracle; two of the fastest bowlers in England were getting every sort of help imaginable from as bad a wicket as ever a first-class game was played on, yet " W.G." remained, and when the ball did not hit some part of his body it hit the middle of his bat, and he scored 66 before something happened that no mortal could have avoided and he was out. The man at the other end during part of this innings, C. E. Green, has described his experience.   " We were both battered about," were his words, " and to this day I carry the mark on my chest where I was struck by a rising ball from Freeman."

With regard to " W.G.'s " bowling in match after match, you find if you examine the scores that he would have been a valuable member of the XI if a run had never come from his bat.

On going through the County Club records it was noticed that all the other counties then in existence were constantly appealing for fixtures with Gloucestershire but being an entirely amateur XI it was not possible for the players to get away from their various vocations; in 1872, however, a request from Yorkshire was complied with and the team visited Sheffield for the first time.   " W.G." had never appeared on this ground before, but Yorkshire folk, keen and enthusiastic then as now, knew all about his achievements and flocked to the ground to see this famous West Countryman.   They saw him score a chanceless 150 and then take 8 Yorkshire wickets in one innings for 33, and 7 in the other for 46 runs.   That fine old

Yorkshireman, Luke Greenwood has, in describing the game to my old friend the late " Old Ebor," one of the best known writers about cricket, said: " Play was stopped on the first day at 5 o'clock. The score was 208 for no wicket. ' W.G.' having made 132 not out and T. G. Matthews 69 not out. I remember that one gentleman sent me a telegram asking me to wire back the state of the game, and I replied, ' We have not got a wicket yet, but are hoping to get one every day.' I got ' W.G.'s ' next day." Greenwood was wrong in saying that T. G. Matthews was 69 not out; he was not playing in this match, and it was " E.M." who opened with his brother and made 89. " In this match," continues Greenwood, " ' W.G.' thwacked me out of the field for six on the legside. There used to be a practice, in those days, of giving a shilling to those who return the balls. An old lady found this one and toddled up to the wicket (as was the custom). She brought the ball to me, and I said, ' Nah, yon's him that hit it; ye, mum, go to him for t'brass.' So she crossed the wicket to ' W.G.' who, much amused, paid the forfeit."

" W.G." never wearied in the field, the sharp edge of his keenness never failed. " He was a real glutton for cricket," wrote the late C. E. Green, who played for three counties— Middlesex, Sussex and Essex. " Nothing could quench his passion for bowling, and I remember once in a match between the Gentlemen of the South and the Players of the South at the Oval, our attack was completely tied up. I. D. Walker, who was captain, came up to ' W.G.' to ask his opinion as to the desirability of a change, and who he should put on. ' W.G.,' who was bowling at the Pavilion end, said quite seriously, ' I tell you what. I'll go on at the other end.' It never occurred to him for a moment that he should be taken off."

As early as 1873 the coming champion drew record crowds wherever he played, and on the occasion of Gloucestershire's first visit to Sheffield during that year no fewer than 23,000 persons watched the play on the three days of the match, while at Nottingham when the Western county first played there, all the factory hands for miles around struck work in order to see the match. In 1878 Gloucestershire's initial appearance at Manchester created unprecedented scenes of enthusiasm, and a newspaper account of the game which has been preserved states:—

" Quite 16,000 were present on the Saturday; they were obliged to have four entrances that day and the people came in such shoals that passing through the turnstiles was difficult; even with four entrances they could not be admitted fast enough, and it is believed that fully 2,000 went round and got over the boards on to the ground without payment. The receipts on that day alone amounted to £400, and it was estimated that altogether more than 28,000 people witnessed the match."

Francis Thompson, the poet, was apparently among the great crowd who saw " W.G." for the first time on that memorable occasion, for he has recorded his impressions in verse : —

> "This day of Seventy Eight, they have
> Come up North against thee,
> This day of Seventy Eight long ago
> The Champion of the Centuries, he
> Cometh up against thee
> With his brethren, everyone a
> Famous foe!
> The long whiskered Doctor, that
> Laughest rules to scorn
> While the bowler pitched against
> Him bans the day he was born,
> And ' G.F.' with his science makes
> The fairest length forlorn;
> They are come up from the West to
> Work thee woe."

Contemporary references to the astonishing success of the Gloucestershire Club during the first few years of its history are highly diverting, and here is a long letter from the correspondence column of an early issue of the " Western Daily Press," signed " X " : —

" I remember that when Gloucestershire presumed to start a County XI your contemporary the ' Standard,' whom ' Punch ' has sometimes likened to an old lady, became almost hysterical. Fancy the ' Old Lady ' on this occasion wiping her spectacles and shrieking, ' What impertinence on the part of these misguided gentlemen of Gloucestershire. But they will find that to compete with the great cricketing counties something more is necessary besides the possession of one good cricketer, meaning, of course, Mr. W. G. Grace.' Your contemporary had scarcely spoken when the Gloucestershire XI began a series of brilliant victories which they brought to a worthy termination last week at the Cheltenham and Clifton College grounds.

" For two years they have been defeated in one match only; namely their opening match of the season when Messrs. E. M. Grace, Miles and Bush were absent, and Messrs. W. G. and G. F. Grace having just returned from Australia had scarcely regained their land legs. But the very complete licking that Gloucestershire administered to Surrey at Cheltenham last week, taking all their first innings wickets for 27 runs, and finishing them off with an innings to spare, more than wiped out the disgrace of this one lost match. Thus the result of the county cricket of the past two years is that Gloucestershire has become the Champion County. We all know how much we owe to the Grace family. The cricket power of those three brothers is something to marvel at. In the last two innings, played on Clifton College ground these wonderful brothers put together no fewer than 434 runs. So much for their skill with the bat; and as for their doings on the other side, I refer you to the printed reports of several of the greatest matches of the season in London, where these words are fast becoming a stereotyped phrase: ' The brothers Grace had a hand in all the wickets.' "

The main purpose of this enthusiastic letter—written over 70 years ago—was to urge the committee of the Gloucestershire Club to consider the necessity of engaging professional players " with a reserve army of professional colts like other great cricketing counties." Our correspondent visualised a time when the muscles of even the great " W.G." would become weak and his joints stiff, and we can only hope that " Mr. X " lived to see that these same muscles and joints produced 22 years later, 1,000 runs in the opening month of the season. Mr. X goes on to say " . . . that cricket is a very desirable game, and worthy of all encouragement. Could not the working classes be induced to give it more attention? There are, I fancy, some Gloucestershire men who would be none the worse off if we could remove them from the tap room to the more bracing atmosphere of Durdham Down, Clifton. I should like to see professional cricket encouraged. As it is, we depend upon the Grace family; and for the future upon whatever the Colleges may chance to provide for us."

It is a strange fact that while " W.G." and his Gloucestershire team were helping materially by their drawing-power to place other counties in a sound financial position, the attendances at Clifton College during this time when they were almost unbeatable were rarely very good, and at Committee meetings the secretary was often instructed to take whatever steps he could to obtain subscribers. The entries in the minute book from 1873 to 1879 indicate that the Club management had constantly to keep down expenses, and members of the team were put on a scale of payment for travelling which must have left them considerably out of pocket by the end of the season. At one meeting there was an animated discussion as to what constituted an out match for Players' expenses; four miles was proposed; seconded and lost. Then followed a motion " That home matches are those which cost the players nothing in the way of hotel expenses; the committee in each case to decide where hotel expenses are necessary." The voting on this motion resulted in a tie, but was carried by the casting vote of the chairman.

When " W.G." became established as a medical practitioner, he was allowed a sum over and above his actual expenses towards paying his assistant; this amount was £20, which some years later, when the number of matches was increased. was raised to £36. There is a popular belief that the " Grand Old Man " made a small fortune out of his cricket for Gloucestershire, but examination of the financial arrangements between him and the Club as recorded in the minute books, shows beyond a shadow of doubt that this belief was a fairy tale and nothing more.

CHAPTER XI

The 80's opened with another visit of an Australian team, this time under the leadership of W. L. Murdoch, who subsequently settled in this country and played for Sussex, and the fact that the tourists beat Gloucestershire at Clifton in August was due as much to the bad fielding of the home team as to the good cricket of the visitors who had been behind on the first innings. In this game " W.G." did not come off with the bat, but shone as a bowler taking 11 wickets for just over 12 runs each; " E.M." scored 65 and 43, while young Fred made 25 in the first innings.

Early in September, 1880, it was arranged that the first Test between England and Australia in this country should be played at Kennington Oval, and for the first time since 1744 three brothers, " E.M.," " W.G.," and " G.F." Grace, appeared in a representative match. The rest of the England XI was composed of A. P. Lucas, W. Barnes, Lord Harris, F. Penn, A. G. Steel, the Hon. A. Lyttleton, Alfred Shaw and F. Morley. Commencing on a Monday, the match attracted no less than 20,814 people who were well rewarded for their enthusiasm, for England ran up a total of 420, of which " W.G." was top scorer with 152, a grand innings which contained only one chance and included twelve 4's. " E.M." contributed 36, but Fred not only made a " duck " in his first innings but, sent in in the second innings, when England wanted only 50-odd to win, bagged a brace. His failure with the bat in what was to prove his last big match was tempered, however, by his magnificent catch to dismiss the giant Bonnor in the first innings. This catch, which is now historic, has been referred to again and again as one of the most remarkable ever made in first-class cricket. Alfred Shaw was bowling to Bonnor, the great hitter, who jumping out caught the ball on the half-volley, and with a mighty hit sent it soaring towards the extreme limit of the Oval enclosure. So high did the ball mount that two runs were scored before it descended, and fell into the safe hands of " G.F.," who had judged his position perfectly. When the distance from the pitch to where Fred Grace made the catch was measured afterwards, it was found to be 115 yards. The Australians were put out for 149, and naturally England with a lead of 271 runs enforced the follow-on, but thanks to a magnificent innings of 153 not out by W. L. Murdoch, the innings defeat was avoided and England were made to bat again, and lost 5 wickets in getting the necessary 57 runs. " W.G." was 9 not out at the finish, but " E.M." like " G.F." failed to score.

Alas, a fortnight after this memorable match Fred Grace died at the early age of 30, and it is generally believed that he contracted a chill as the result of sleeping in a damp bed; congestion of the lungs set in, and his virile life was at an end. One of the saddest tasks the Gloucestershire Committee ever had to undertake during the early years of the Club's history was the passing of a resolution recording " their deep and heartfelt sympathy with Mrs. Grace on the incomparable loss she had sustained by the death of her son, Mr. G. F. Grace." It is, of course, impossible to realise how greatly the passing of this young man was deplored throughout the country. Few cricketers had achieved more universal popularity, his charm of personality, as much as his brilliance in each phase of the game, endearing him as much to the sporting people of the North and South of England as at home in the West. Mrs. Grace in acknowledging the Committee's resolution of sympathy, wrote: —

" It is certainly of some consolation and very gratifying to me to know that dearest Fred was appreciated by the Committee and his numerous friends, but they can have no conception of his real worth at home. His many gentle virtues added to his noble character endeared him in an extraordinary degree to us all. To know him was to love him."

" A brilliant batsman, an exceptionally fine bowler, great in the field, and a genial sort withal," is how Fred Grace was described by one of his biographers, and like his brothers he never missed the chance of a match. At an age when most boys are content to watch fast bowling on a bumpy wicket, he was standing up to it fearlessly, taking the hard knocks without any fuss. A contemporary of his remembers him as a lad of 14, tall for his age, rather slim, very dark and " the image of his mother." He played his first important game

G. F. GRACE

for the South of the Thames v. the North of the Thames, in 1866 when not yet 16, while two years later he was playing for England against the M.C.C. at Lord's. He appears, however, to have taken longer to accustom himself to first-class cricket than did his brothers, but in 1870 he jumped to the fore with a fine innings of 189 for the Gentlemen of the South against the Gentlemen of the North, his stand with I. D. Walker, who made 179, lasting over seven hours. Later on he found time to play in a variety of important matches; in 1872 he gave a wonderful all-round display against Notts, scoring 115 and 72 not out, and taking 7 wickets for 43. In the same season for the United South v. the United North, at Northampton, he took all ten wickets. For several seasons Fred captained and managed the United South of England team, and toured the country with it. In 1873-4 he went to Australia with " W.G.," and took a prominent part in the success of the tour, his innings of 154 against Tasmania standing for some years as the highest score by an Englishman in Australia; he also made a brilliant 112 in another game. Four days after their return from Australia, " G.F." and " W.G." turned out for Clifton against Thornbury. Fred scored 123, but Gilbert could only amass 25. Although the Champion and his younger brother usually appeared on the same side, there were times when they played against each other. This happened in a Surrey v. M.C.C. match—qualification rules in those days were more free and easy than now, and in order to strengthen the Surrey XI Fred was made a member. Scoring 60 runs and taking 5 wickets for 24, he fully justified his election to this august club.

In his last season—1880—Fred's best innings for Gloucestershire was 83 against Middlesex at Lord's, a match in which rain rescued the home county from a probable innings defeat. " G.F.'s " aggregate of 320 in county games that season was second only to " W.G." who totalled 605.

Richard Daft had a very high opinion of Fred Grace and referred to his style as a batsman being worth any young cricketer's while to copy, while as an outfield he considered him the most magnificent he ever saw. Some of his catches were, in Daft's opinion, truly marvellous.

Between 1870 and the time of his death, Fred Grace scored 3,216 runs for Gloucestershire in 105 completed innings which gave him an average of 30.6. These figures included four centuries, all scored, strange to relate, at Clifton; his highest effort being 180 not out against Yorkshire in 1875. The loss Gloucestershire cricket sustained by his tragic death is immeasurable, in fact " W.G." went so far as to say that not only Gloucestershire but England had lost a great player whose place would not be easy to fill.

CHAPTER XII

1880 was another good year for Gloucestershire who once again suffered only one defeat, and that at the hands of Surrey; their fielding, however, was very far from the old Gloucestershire standard and was a deciding factor in their match with the Australians at Clifton. " W.G.," batting as consistently as ever, headed the county averages, a total of 605 runs giving him an average of over 43. " E.M.'s " batting, on the other hand, fell off decidedly, and with 32 as his best score his average was a modest 14. The only three-figure innings played by " W.G." for his county was a match-winning 106 against Lancashire at Clifton, when for once he did not open the batting but went in at No. 7. The following year Gloucestershire, although suffering from a lack of first-class bowling, managed to win 6 matches and lose only 2, but the gap created by Fred's sudden death was a wide one, and not easy to fill. " W.G.," although scoring only one hundred—a brilliant 182 v. Notts—increased his aggregate to 720, but his average was slightly lower. " E.M." showed a welcome return to form with the bat, his average rising from 14 to 27; while as a bowler " W.G." enjoyed a big personal success against Middlesex at Lord's, taking 7 first-innings wickets for 30 runs besides scoring 64. For the Gentlemen at the Oval the Champion added yet another hundred to his growing list of centuries off the Professionals' bowling. It was a fine innings of exactly 100, made out of 167 for 3, and was followed up by another excellent piece of bowling in the second innings when he captured 7 wickets for 61.

1882, which will be remembered as the most disastrous season experienced by Gloucestershire since the formation of the Club, was also a memorable one for " W.G." who failed to reach three figures during the summer for the first time since 1867. Nevertheless he still topped the batting, and had the satisfaction of taking more wickets (74) than any other Gloucestershire bowler. ". E.M.," on the other hand, had quite recovered his lost batting form, and scored centuries against Lancashire and Somerset.

It was during one of the matches against the Australians at Clifton this season that G. J. Bonnor, the hitter, on being dismissed for a small score, was asked the manner of his dismissal. " I was talked out by one of the fielders," was his reply.

1883 was another poor year for Gloucestershire cricket, despite the fact that " W.G." finished third in the first-class averages with a total of 1,352 runs, which once again included only one hundred. Bad as had been the previous two seasons for Gloucestershire, 1884 was without doubt the worst in the Club's history, for out of a dozen games only one ended in a win; yet at Clifton, that doleful year, the county played brilliantly against the Australian team, which a few days later scored 551 against England at the Oval, " W.G." scoring 116 not out in a total of 301, while in the second innings J. H. Brain made 108 out of 230 for 2.

As far back as 1873 a wise old cricket lover had prophesied that the time would come when those who were carrying all before them would lose their form, and had urged the county to look out for professional recruits. Unfortunately, this advice was not acted upon until the county's resources were sadly deteriorated. G. F. Grace was dead; Midwinter had returned to Australia; and W. O. Moberley and R. F. Miles had dropped out; thus it was only late in the season when the Universities and Public Schools were on holiday that Gloucestershire could put a really representative team in the field. There were during this unsatisfactory period some very notable recruits, both amateur and professional, the latter including three old friends, W. A. Woof, Fred Roberts and Jack Painter, three fine cricketers who had the ill-luck to be at their best when the county's fortunes were at their lowest ebb. Yet Woof and Roberts were absolutely in the front rank of England's bowlers and achieved many bowling triumphs.

All three of " W.G.'s " centuries in 1884 were made at the expense of the Australian team; the first was 101 for the M.C.C. at Lord's, he and A. G. Steel (134) adding 124 for the fourth wicket while in addition the Doctor took 7 wickets; the second hundred was an almost fautless 107 for the Gentlemen of England at the Oval, and the third and last 116 not out for Gloucestershire at Clifton.

During the 80's " W.G." saw many of his old friends pass out of the game, but " E.M.," J. A. Bush and Frank Townsend remained and others who came along included W. W. F. Pullen, O. G. Radcliffe, H. V. Page, the father of the late D. A. C. Page who was killed in a car crash at the end of 1936, and the three professionals already mentioned. O. G. Radcliffe, who had the distinction of playing for three counties — Somerset, Wiltshire and Gloucestershire—was a most attractive batsman, with a c urious stroke which came along every now and then and took the field completely by surprise, for the ball sometimes mounted high in the air between point and cover, and sometimes pitched over the boundary. " O.G." was, however, somewhat erratic and there were long gaps between his big scores; he is best remembered for a glorious 117 against Kent at Bristol, which helped to pull the Western County out of a bad position and pave the way to a fine victory.

J. H. Brain was a Clifton College boy who afterwards captained Oxford, and the best of his many good innings for Gloucestershire was his 108 against the Australians on his old school ground in 1884. He was also one of the many brilliant fielders the county has had, and well remember his famous catch at Clifton College, close to the Chapel, which ended Bobby Abel's innings at 99. It has always been said that " W.G." gave the Surrey crack this one to hit and get his hundred but it was not so; the Big Doctor was out for his wicket, and Bobby, like many another famous batsmen, fell into the trap.

W. W. F. Pullen was another attractive batsman when well set, but like many other amateurs who could not play regularly he was usually in too much of a hurry to get off the mark, and it was only occasionally that he was seen at his best. There was one season, however, in 1884, when he was top of the batting averages for Gloucestershire and against Middlesex at Cheltenham played the best innings of his career, scoring 164.

The first professional to play for Gloucestershire was Hall, the second was Midwinter, and the third, W. A. Woof, whose name is a household word in sport at Cheltenham and who captured 750 wickets for 17 runs each during his career for the county which lasted from 1880-92. Woof was a left-hander with a rare command over length and spin, and for some years was one of the very best bowlers in England. It was always

a great pleasure to meet " W.A." at Cheltenham during the
Festival and accompany him to look over his kennel of fox-
terriers at his house close to the College.

In the Minute Book of the County Committee, dated April
28th, 1881, appears the following entry:—

> " Proposed by W. G. Grace, seconded by J. F. Norris,
> that £2 10s. d. be allowed to J. Painter if he comes to play
> in a colt's match at Bedminster."

It was the following year, however, that Jack Painter commenced service with Gloucestershire; he hailed from the North
and was recommended as a good all-rounder. Curiously
enough " W.G." gave him little chance to prove his worth as
a bowler, and H. V. Page has given as an explanation for this
that during the Cheltenham Week Jack's friends tried to coerce
the Doctor into putting him on to bowl by shouting " Painter!
Painter! " The older generation will perhaps remember the
great partnership between J. H. Brain and Painter against
Surrey at Clifton in 1884, when the amateur scored 143, and
Jack 133. In this game, although Surrey totalled 464,
Gloucestershire beat it by 20.

Fred Roberts played for Gloucestershire from 1887 till 1902,
and he could probably tell as many stories as anyone of the
captain who so often told him to keep his arm up. How Fred
came to play for Gloucestershire has been the subject of typical examples of cricket fiction, invented to give spice to a yarn,
but here are his own words which should suffice : —

> " While I was in Sussex, W. G. N. Wyatt who was then
> in the County XI said he would write to Mr. Grace about
> me; but he forgot to do so until the following season. Then
> " W.G." had me to bowl to him at the Oval, before the
> Gents v. Players match, and I suppose I must have satisfied
> him for shortly afterwards I had a telegram from him on
> the day before the Yorkshire match, to go to Dewsbury.
> Here I took 7 wickets in each innings."

Fourteen wickets in his first match! Not many bowlers have
had a more successful introduction to first-class cricket
than this; as a rule, bowlers have to feel their way, but here
was a raw recruit who bowled at a great pace and made the
ball swing away to leg in a manner that was not common in
those days.

" W.G." was, for a great part of his career brilliant in any position of the field, and it was said by his many contemporaries that nobody ever saw him miss a catch. He will be remembered, generally, at point, and it will therefore surprise many to know that both he and his brother, " E.M.," were expert wicket-keepers. Often in their young days they kept to each other's bowling, wearing gloves only, and among the trophies treasured at Park House, Thornbury, is a ball mounted on a silver stand which was presented to " E.M." for his wicket-keeping in Australia. Another fact which will astonish many is that " W.G." once kept wicket in a Test Match against Australia. This was the notable occasion—the only one in a match of importance—when every member of the England XI had a turn at bowling; the last to be called upon was the Hon. Alfred Lyttleton, the wicket-keeper, and when he took off his gloves and pads " W.G." put them on, and caught Midwinter, who was playing for Australia. Lyttleton, bowling lobs, took 4 wickets for 19 runs, and this Test which was played at the Oval ended in a draw, Australia scoring 551 to England's 345, a total which did not seem probable when 8 wickets had fallen for 186, but which was made possible by the batting of Scotton and W. W. Read who added 151 runs for the 9th wicket, a record partnership by England for that wicket in Tests and one which has yet to be broken.

In 1885, Gloucestershire improved on their record of the past three summers, winning 6 matches and losing 7, a record which was really very satisfactory seeing that " E.M." did not play in a single match. " W.G." however was in splendid form scoring 1,034 runs for the excellent average of 43. The counties whose bowling suffered most at his hands were Middlesex, against whom he made 69 and 54 at Lord's, and 221 not out at Clifton; Surrey, 104, 55 and 19 not out; and Yorkshire, 132, 54 and 34. In the two games with Middlesex he also took 16 wickets. Outside county cricket " W.G." made another century for the Gentlemen, this time at Scarborough.

The improvement which Gloucestershire had shown in 1885 was, unfortunately, not maintained during the following season and the county had the humiliating experience of finishing one from the bottom of the Championship Table. " W.G.," for once, failed to bat with his usual confidence and did not score a single hundred; as a bowler he took 60 wickets, but at an increased cost. " E.M." returned to the team, but he also accomplished nothing outstanding. Apart from championship games " W.G." batted well, adding four more centuries to his ever increasing list, three of which were made at the expense of the Australians and in the third and final Test at the Oval he made his best score of the season and incidentally his highest against Australia, a grand innings of 170 out of 216, including 22 4's. In this match he and Scotton, Prince of Stonewallers, put on 170 for the 1st wicket, before the latter was out for 34; this was a record stand for these games. For Gloucestershire against the Tourists at Clifton he accomplished one of his best all-round performances scoring 110 in the 2nd innings after taking 7 first innings wickets for 67, which enabled Gloucestershire to lead on the first innings. His third hundred against the visitors was 148 for the Gentlemen of England at the Oval, he and W. H. Patterson scoring 104 for the first wicket .

CHAPTER XIII

For several years the Gloucestershire Committee had been endeavouring to find a suitable ground in Bristol for their headquarters, but owing to lack of financial backing they had been unable to take advantage of several excellent opportunities which had occurred. At last, in 1887, their attention was drawn to a site at Ashley Down; this position seemed at the time a long way off, and was criticised on that account, but the price being reasonable and the ground level, it was decided at the December meeting to appoint Messrs. E. G. Clarke, J. W. Arrowsmith and H. W. Beloe to treat with the owner and tenant for rental or purchase " with permission to ascertain if any person or persons would purchase the whole 25 acres on the understanding that the Club was allowed to take any portion up to 12 or 13 acres at a rateable price and terms (either purchaser or rental on a lease with option to purchase) to be settled by some competent independent person."

Here we have the first steps taken to secure the ground which is known to cricketers of several generations, a ground which has for many the happiest of memories and one which will always be associated with the name of W. G. Grace, for it was here that he achieved his crowning triumph, the completion of his 100th century, in 1895, and also one of his greatest scores for Gloucestershire, 301 in that never to be forgotten Bank Holiday match against Sussex the following year.

At a meeting in January, 1888, it was resolved " that schemes be drawn providing for the acquisition of the ground by one or more of which the County Club should have the sole and exclusive control of the portion to be set aside for cricket and athletic purposes." A month later it was further resolved " that it is desirable for a limited company to be formed at once to purchase the twenty-six acres at Ashley Down now under offer by the representatives of H. W. Green, the style of the company to be ' The Gloucestershire County Ground Co. Limited.' " The relationship of the club to the company is set out in full in the Minutes and Messrs. Clarke, Arrowsmith, Beloe and Arthur Robinson were requested to purchase the ground at the price offered—£6,500. Thus the Gloucestershire County Ground Company was duly formed, and Dr. W. G. Grace was appointed as the first member of the county club to serve as a director on the board of management.

All these steps took place early in 1888, yet so rapid was the progress in getting the land enclosed that it was found possible to play a Colts match there in the following May when the formal opening ceremony was performed. " W.G." spent so much time on the ground during the work of construction that he became almost part of the landscape, and just as his father had for years, as one of his most fervent desires, a county ground for Gloucestershire, so had the Champion, and here were his hopes being realised.

Those of us who were privileged to have the right to play there from the start will remember that the portion upon which Bristol Rugby Club and the Clifton Association Club played football was divided from the cricket area by a hedge, and that down in the corner was a cowshed in which we used to shelter when it rained. One occasion comes to mind when a match with a theatrical company was so much interrupted that the artistes from Prince's Theatre, Bristol, gave us a first-class variety entertainment until the storm had passed.

It must have been a proud moment for Dr. Grace when, on May 4th, 1888, he went out with W. Troup to open the county innings against the Colts, and it is to be regretted that he did not open the ground with a century; as it happened he was bowled for 35. The County XI in this game included three of his old comrades of the '70's, " E.M.," Frank Townsend and J. A. Bush, while his eldest son, who became known as " W.G. Junior," then a lad of fourteen, was also in the side. The Colts team also included a well-known local figure in H. W. Chard, of the Schoolmasters, one of the few to reach double figures. He was a fine all-rounder, and in 1889 played several times for the county, being concerned with D. L. Evans in a big stand against Sussex at Brighton; he devoted much of his life to club cricket, and Bristol Cricket Association in particular. W. H. Hale, of Knowle, had the distinction of playing county cricket and county rugger for both Somerset and Gloucestershire; Edwin Fenner of the Y.M.C.A. was one of the hardest hitters ever seen in Bristol club cricket and a

great rugger three-quarter for Bristol and Gloucestershire, and
F. C. Bracher, one of the best stylists and fielders in local
cricket. It was by his fielding that Bracher first aroused
" W.G.'s " notice. He was playing in a club match on the
County Ground, fielding opposite the pavilion inside which
" W.G." was watching the game. Presently the ball came
soaring in his direction; Bracher stood on the edge of the grass,
made the catch, threw the ball up—a habit of his—and
stepped back on to the track. The question then arose as to
whether the catch had been made before or after the fielder
had stepped over the boundary. In the midst of the dispute
" W.G." came out and settled the argument. " The catch was
made right enough, and a good 'un, too," he said, and turning
to Bracher he asked him if he could play in the trial match
the following Thursday. Bracher played in that match, which
I remember well, for being one of the umpires, I gave " E.M."
out to the first ball bowled—an L.B.W. decision and a bad
one, which put me out of favour with the Coroner for some
time.

Harking back to the season of 1887, we find that although
" W.G." returned to his best form, hitting up five hundreds in
county games alone, Gloucestershire failed disastrously again,
having only one win to set off against nine defeats. As an
all-rounder the Big Doctor stood supreme, heading the county
batting with the fine record of 1,405 runs for an average of
63, and taking over 60 wickets. So consistent was his batting
that summer that a brief resumé of it here would not be out
of place. At Brighton he made 47 and 51 against Sussex,
following this up with 113 off Middlesex at Lord's. Against
Surrey at Moreton-in-the-Marsh he was top scorer with 58
in a total of 97, the only man able to stand up to the bowling
of G. Jones; from there he proceeded to Gloucester where he
scored 275 for once out (183 in the second innings) against the
strong Yorkshire attack, while in the return game at Dewsbury
he made 97 and 20. During the month of August he registered
92 v. Somerset; 32 not out v. Sussex; 113 not out v. Notts;
63 and 31 v. Middlesex; but his greatest success was his two
centuries (101 and 103 not out) against Kent at Clifton.
" E.M.'s " aggregate of 552 was very small in comparison, and
being the next highest to " W.G.'s," showed how much the
county depended on the Champion.

1887 concluded for " W.G." on a somewhat humorous
note, for, during the Scarborough Festival, cricket had come

to an end early one afternoon, so the M.C.C. team challenged
the Yorkshire XI to an Association Football match. " W.G."
played half-back and was the star turn of his side, one of
the two M.C.C. goals coming from his accurately placed
corner kick, and the other from an opening in which he got
past Lord Hawke and Tom Emmett in grand style. The
game, which was great fun, ended under the Rugby rules,
" W.G." scoring the winning try.

Whereas in 1887 " W.G.'s " batting triumphs were almost
the only creditable feature of Gloucestershire cricket, 1888 saw
the county make a distinct advance at all points despite the
fact that the Champion's record fell far below that of the
previous season. The Gloucestershire captain played three
big innings for the county, but apart from these did nothing
at all outstanding; yet Gloucestershire rose from 8th to 4th
place in the Championship, passing such prominent counties
as Lancashire, Notts, Middlesex and Sussex. Five matches
were won and the same number lost, while outside these games
two brilliant victories were gained over the Australians. The
season being terribly wet it was hardly to be expected that
" W.G." would be able to approach his form of the previous
summer, and under the circumstances his record of 900 runs
for an average of 36 was really very creditable. His highest
score was made against Sussex at Brighton, a fine effort of
215 which included 22 fours and was almost faultless, while
against Yorkshire at Clifton he once again accomplished the
feat of a hundred in each innings scoring 148 and 153, his fine
batting in the second innings enabling Gloucestershire to draw.
To the two victories over the Australians he contributed
materially by taking 4 wickets for 24 and scoring 51 at Clifton,
while at Cheltenham he made a brilliant 92. " E.M." showed
a great falling off on his previous record, his average dropping
from 23 to 12.

Although " W.G.'s " batting record for the county in 1889
remained stationary, Gloucestershire ended the '80's with yet
another indifferent season which might well have been worse
had not rain saved them in two drawn games. " E.M." went
from bad to worse, his aggregate of a mere 183 runs giving
him the meagre average of 10, but as a bowler he had the
distinction of heading the county averages, his 10 wickets
costing just under 16 runs apiece; his best performance was
4 for 26 against Yorkshire at Gloucester, an effort which gave
the home county a well deserved victory by 93 runs.

CHAPTER XIV

During the season 1890, the Champion had the unusual experience of just missing his century three times in a fortnight, while in May he carried his bat right through an innings of 231 against Kent at Maidstone for 109 bringing his total of hundreds to 93. With only seven more to reach his goal and achieve what no other cricketer had ever done before, it must have been very disappointing to him to miss three centuries after getting into the 90's. At Manchester, on July 24, on a bad wicket against such bowlers as Barlow, Watson, Mold, Baker and Hewetson, he batted superbly for 94, when his ancient rival, A. N. Hornby, the G.O.M. of Lancashire cricket, caught him. The Lancashire captain must have been very pleased with himself for, if current gossip is to be believed, the two had been the keenest opponents for over 20 years, and not always the best of friends. The state of the Old Trafford wicket during this match can be gauged from the fact that a powerful batting side, with Frank Sugg, Albert Ward and Dick Barlow, was dismissed by Woof and Roberts for 60 runs.

In the return game at Clifton on August 7th, " W.G." batted beautifully until he reached 90, and then fell to a wonder catch on the leg-side. Between these two matches, Gloucestershire met Yorkshire at Dewsbury, and " W.G." displayed his usual partiality for their bowling for opening the second innings with Gloucestershire 135 behind, the loss of three good wickets failed to disturb him and after helping James Cranston to add 188 for the 4th wicket, he fell an l.b.w. victim to Bobby Peel still 2 short of his hundred. This game, by the way, was won by Gloucestershire after a victory for Yorkshire had seemed inevitable, and it was " W.G.'s " wonderful steadiness and skill which made it possible.

Dr. E. M. Grace was not so fortunate as was his younger brother in avoiding the unenviable distinction of " spectacles," and after nearly forty years of first-class cricket bagged a brace against Surrey at Cheltenham. It must have been a bad moment in the old man's life when George Lohmann took a snick from " E.M." low down in the slips with one hand in the second innings and he must have thought on his way back to the pavilion that it was time he gave up his place in the team to a younger man. He did not, however, give up, and there were still a few more triumphs for him before he finally parted company with those old friends of his who were still in the team. In June, 1890, at Gloucester, " E.M." and " W.G." opened the innings against Kent, and the Champion was bowled in the first over by " Nutty " Martin for a " duck," but " E.M.," then in his fiftieth year, went on to score a wonderful 96, and one can see him in imagination standing up to the bowling of Martin, Wright and the two Hearnes (Alec and George), ready for each delivery with his bat off the ground, sloping slightly toward the wicket and both eyes on the bowler. It was not my good fortune to see the Coroner in his best days, but as far as I know he never changed his methods, and as he played in the '80's and '90's so he played all through his career with a complete disregard of the conventions. He was like a cat on hot bricks, full of antics, pretending there was a run when there was no chance, getting the ball here and there with curious jabs and pushes; sometimes raising a leg and steering a fast one just wide of the wicket-keeper to the boundary; and every now and then cracking one for four with a lusty swing of the bat. How the crowd enjoyed " E.M.'s " cricket! It was so entirely different from the sober, methodical artistry of his brother and so full of the festive element and indescribable mannerisms which made his play unlike that of any other player the game has ever known. It was while " E.M." was batting that a singular accident occurred to one of the Kent players, C. J. M. Fox, who, when fielding fairly close in at point, stooped very quickly to gather the ball from a hit by W. W. F. Pullen, dropped on the ground and rolled about evidently in great pain. " E.M." ran to him, and " W.G." hurried out of the pavilion. Whatever was wrong, the injured man was lucky in having two doctors in attendance. The spectators wondered what had happened; they wondered still more when they saw " E.M." sit on Fox's head, while " W.G." seized his arm, placed one foot on his body and began to pull. Fox had dislocated his shoulder and the two doctors had to adopt rough and ready methods to get it back. Only one other similar accident has been recorded, and curiously enough C. J. M. Fox was again the victim, this time against Gloucestershire on the County Ground, Bristol, but on this occasion " W.G." was not playing and " E.M." had to obtain the services of two Kent men to assist in putting it back again.

There must be many who remember the Bank Holiday match at the County Ground, Bristol, in 1890, which is memorable as the last time the famous brothers opened the Gloucestershire innings, as they used to in the '70's, with a century partnership. Sussex had provided the Bank Holiday attraction at Bristol for a good many years and what wonderful crowds we had when the weather was fine, for although Gloucestershire had no interest in the competition for Championship honours, it had no effect on the average cricket enthusiast for " W.G." was still an irresistible attraction and on this bright sunny day in August, 1890, several thousands flocked to the ground. What a roar of delight went up when " W.G." came down the steps followed by " E.M." on their way out to as perfect a wicket as John Spry ever prepared. Sussex had some good men in the team at that time; little W. G. Quaife, named after the Doctor, was then beginning his career; C. Aubrey Smith, the stage and screen actor, known as " Round-the-Corner" Smith because of his peculiar run up to the wicket; the two Hides, Arthur and Jesse; Harry Butt, the wicket-keeper; and Walter Humphreys. These were among the fielders waiting to get to grips with " W.G." and his brother on this unforgettable Bank Holiday. Unfortunately for the visitors neither the curly lobs of Walter Humphreys nor the varied attack of seven other Sussex bowlers could succeed in separating the brothers Grace until the total had reached 117. Both batted with confidence and the delight of the crowd knew no bounds as the score mounted. " W.G." was the first to go, bowled by Arthur Hide for 46. He had batted more sedately than usual and had, no doubt, watched with pride and pleasure his elder brother hitting hard and often at the other end, reminding him of the days of their glowing youth. This was their last big stand for Gloucestershire and because of that I have lingered over the match which is still fresh in my memory though so many years have passed since I cheered with the rest when the century went up and when " E.M." returned to the pavilion. We did not know then that we should never again see the Big and Little Doctors take part in a century stand, but it was so, for although they opened the innings many times during the following few seasons, and occasionally gave the side a good start, this was their last big stand together.

It is interesting to note the engagements of professionals in the '90's and to compare the economical rates of pay with which they had to be content with to those of to-day. In April, 1890, it was resolved to engage W. Murch and J. W. Stinchcombe as bowlers at the County Ground, Bristol, and happily for them they were able to add to their small salary by working for the County Ground Company at 6d. per hour. Bill Murch, although rather a disappointing cricketer, was a favourite with " W.G." and had a very good run for several seasons without striking the form that many good judges, including his captain, looked for. There is no entry in the minutes regarding the engagement of Jack Board, who was one of the discoveries of the 1890 Colts' match, and who owed his introduction to first-class cricket entirely to the judgment of " W.G." in spotting a good youngster in the rough. Not often was that judgment at fault, but there are two instances when the Champion was obviously wrong. The first occurred when Nichol was allowed to leave the county and play for Somerset, and the second was in not accepting the application of S. P. Kinneir, a Wiltshire lad who qualified for Warwickshire and rendered that county splendid service as an opening bat. It must, however, be remembered that " W.G." had a strong regard for amateurs and held the view that a preponderance of professionals in first-class cricket was not desirable in the interests of the game, and here are some of his views on the subject:—

" There is another thing I am afraid of: that is, that cricket will be made too much of a business, like football, with the consequence that none but professionals will be seen playing. That, I hope, will not come in our time; but there is that probability to be faced.

" Should such a condition of affairs occur, betting and all kindred evils will follow in its wake, and instead of the game being followed up for love, it will simply be a matter of £ s d."

This was the great man's view 58 years ago, and much as I dislike suggesting that anything could be wrong with what " W.G." said about cricket, I must confess that in this particular instance his words were neither wise nor well chosen.

Painted by A. S. Wortley   *By special permission of the*
Committee of the M.C.C

DR. W. G. GRACE

The game of cricket might well have remained as obscure as folk lore or Morris dancing but for the interest of " the nobility and gentry," and their desire to find some outlet for their love of gambling, which had been restricted by the abolition of bull-baiting, cock-fighting and prize-fights. The early history of cricket is very largely made up of matches for substantial sums, challenges being made and accepted in much the same way as for a cock fight, and these gambling events served to arouse the interest of the sporting public. In time it was found that the game was good enough without the gamble, and so it will always be, I am sure, whether played by amateurs or professionals.

" W.G.'s " preference for a team of amateurs is well known. It is known, too, that he had a greater liking for public school and university recruits than club cricketers from Bristol, Gloucester and other parts of the county, a policy which led to a lot of trouble, not only with members of the committee but club cricketers generally. It is probable that the " Old Man " was right, for he kept in very close touch with local cricket and had plenty of chances to spot an outstanding player if there was one about, but his view was not the general view and he was greatly upset when his methods of recruiting the county side were discussed in committee. It is to be regretted that the secretary was more brief than usual in recording what happened at a memorable committee meeting in 1892. Here is an exact copy of an incident which led to " W.G.'s " resignation as captain of the team:—

" Re the selection of players:—

F. Lawrence spoke.
A. Robinson spoke.
E. J. Taylor spoke.
H. Grace spoke.
E. G. Clarke spoke.
W. G. Grace spoke.

But no resolution was put to the meeting."

It is clear from what followed that some members of the committee were not satisfied with the arrangement that gave " W.G." the first and last word as to who should play for the county, and one would like to know who were for and who against the captain in this controversy, but there is now no means of clearing up this point. As far back as 1873 the committee by resolution delegated the task of selecting the team to the captain, and it is certain that " W.G." would have no interference with what he regarded as his established right. The discussion probably opened with a mild and carefully expressed suggestion, but must have developed into a heated debate, things being said which upset the Doctor; for at the next meeting his resignation from the Committee and captaincy were announced, the secretary's entry being, as usual, just bare facts:—

" H. W. Beloe explained matters to the meeting, when it was resolved:

" The Committee have heard with much regret of the resignation of Dr. W. G. Grace from the Committee and captaincy of the XI, believing he has taken this course in consequence of what took place at the last meeting on December 9th.

" They beg to remind him of the assurance then given him that the Committee did not wish to take any action distasteful or antagonistic to him, and as they still have the same confidence in his captaincy now as previous to the meeting of December 9th, they request him, in the interests of the county XI and cricket generally, to reconsider his determination and withdraw his resignation."

This was not the only result of the trouble: at the next meeting of the Committee, a letter of resignation was read from Mr. H. W. Beloe, the Chairman. These were evidently troublous times for the management. But very little was heard outside of what was taking place; indeed, to all but a few this chapter in the history of Gloucestershire cricket will be entirely new. A resolution urging Mr. Beloe, the Chairman, to withdraw his resignation was passed, and with regard to the captain it was further resolved:—

" That the Committee received with much regret the letter from Dr. W. G. Grace resigning the captaincy of the Club, and while declining to accept the same, decided to adjourn the meeting to a date when it would be convenient for Dr. Grace to attend.

" That in the meantime an endeavour be made to ascertain whether, if it be the general wish of the Committee, Dr. Grace would be prepared to concur in appointing a selection committee as a means of preventing in future the recurrence of such observations as were referred to in the Doctor's letter."

Happily peace was restored. Mr. Beloe withdrew his resignation, and at a subsequent meeting the following letter from " W.G." was read:—

" After due consideration, as it is the wish of the Committee, I will withdraw my letter of resignation. I do this simply for the sake of our county cricket. With regard to the selection committee, I will have nothing to do with it. I do not think it will help us to win matches or that it would work at all satisfactorily. What is more, most if not all of the playing members are of my opinion."

How characteristic is this letter of " W.G. ": no beating about the bush. What he thought, he said, frankly and unreservedly; and happily, the Committee accepting his terms —for the time being, at any rate—peace, so far as the Committee was concerned, prevailed. Unfortunately, however, there was a growing discontent outside the Club with the Doctor's dictatorship in the matter of team selection, which was frequently alluded to at club dinners and other gatherings; and at one of these dinners at which " W.G." was a guest, he departed from his usual practice and made a speech, replying to his critics, and he didn't mince matters. This speech aroused a storm of controversy in the newspapers, the late Mr. George Bradbeer, captain of the Y.M.C.A., taking up the cause of club cricketers and publishing a very aggressive rejoinder to the Gloucestershire captain, blaming the management because in four years the county team had only won 8 games for which the policy of not recruiting club cricketers was held responsible. But it afterwards became obvious that " W.G.'s " critics were wrong, and that a county team could never be maintained by young men who could only play occasionally. It is probable, too, that Dr. Grace was right in considering that few, if any, club players then taking part in local cricket were up to county form; for his experience with the few club recruits he had tried had been far from satisfactory, and as far as amateurs were concerned, this has been the experience of those who have managed the county XI since " W.G.'s " time. Midway through the '90's, however, there came a wonderful change in the club's fortunes: " W.G." gathered round him a brilliant band of amateurs, obtained not from the clubs but the Varsities and public schools.   It is, no doubt, the experience of all great men to run foul of popular opinion now and then, and Dr. W. G. Grace certainly did during the first few years of the '90's, but in 1895 he was able to turn the tables on his critics by his own amazing triumphs and the form of those newcomers who, in the years to follow, were able to revive Gloucestershire's failing fortunes.

Whatever doubts there may be as to " W.G.'s " best season, there can be no question as to which was his worst—1891— for in 22 innings for the county he could only aggregate 440 runs, while his average of 20.95 reached low water mark. In the general averages, too, the Champion dropped to 19th place, a very sad experience for him. A bad leg sprain partly explained his failure, but as this accident did not occur until mid-season, there was undoubtedly another cause for this loss of form. The summer passed without any addition to " W.G.'s " long list of centuries, and we have the unfamiliar sequence of seeing him give up his time-honoured place at the head of the batting on several occasions and go in 3rd, and 4th wicket down, and even lower. " E.M.," who scored only 15 runs less than his brother, was second in the county batting table, with an average of 15, showing the terrible state of Gloucestershire's batting resources.

It is interesting to note that in this, his worst season for the county, " W.G." still rose to the occasion at Lord's. The match was North v. South (Rylott's Benefit), and against such redoubtable bowlers as Dick Pougher, Peel, Attewell, Barnes and Flowers, he scored 61 in 70 minutes. This match, by the way, had a very special interest for Gloucestershire supporters, as it was the fixture which introduced Jack Board to first-class cricket. He had played for the Colts against the county in 1890, and for the county against the Colts the following year, and was waiting to hear from " W.G." A telegram arrived, but it was not to play for Gloucestershire, but for the South against the North at Lord's. Board, however, knew nothing of this when the wire arrived, for all " W.G." told him was to go at once to Mrs. Grace at Stapleton, and she said that the Doctor wished him to be at Lord's on Monday morning. She gave him £2 and full instructions for the journey, even to the amount he was to pay for his cab from Paddington to Lord's. It must have been a wonderful experience for a young man who had never been to London before, and a proud moment when Dr. Grace took him round to the professionals' room at Lord's and, introducing him to the Players, told them to look after him. There is not, as far as I know, another instance in the whole history of the game, of a young and untried player going from the humblest of local cricket to a match of such importance, but Jack had a big heart as well as big horny hands, and he stood up to the bowling of Sharp and Lohmann of Surrey, Martin of Kent, and Ferris the Australian like an old timer, and we may be sure that " W.G." was very pleased with his protegé. A week later, Board was in the Gloucestershire team and, as everyone knows, became one of the best wicket-keepers in England, and so good a batsman that for many years he was always near the top of the averages.

In the winter of 1891 " W.G." paid a second visit to Australia, this time as a member of Lord Sheffield's team; and this tour is said to have restored much of the confidence which he had lost as the result of his indifferent form in the English season of 1891. During this tour he was out in the first over in a match at Adelaide, to what was described as the best catch ever seen in Australia. The fielder, J. Reedman, ran 25 yards and then, jumping, caught the ball with one hand just as it seemed certain to land among the spectators.

It is recorded that " W.G." received £3,000 for the trip which altogether cost Lord Sheffield £16,000; and according to Alfred Shaw, who acted as manager, resulted in his Lordship being £2,000 out of pocket.

The years 1891-94 were for Gloucestershire years of extreme ill-luck, for when they were not bottom of the championship they were very near it. After his poor record of 1891, " W.G.'s" total of over 800 runs the following year seemed very good; but once again he failed to reach three figures, his best effort being an excellent 99 in the second innings against Sussex at Gloucester. " E.M.", although his average remained the same, managed to equal his brother's record of 440 runs the previous season, but neither of them accomplished anything with the ball. In 1893 W. G. Grace, Junior, made his first appearance for Gloucestershire against Middlesex at Clifton, but his record of 0 and 11 was not impressive. He played in several other games that year with little or no success. 1893 saw W.G., Senior, score his first hundred for three years, a flawless 128 for the M.C.C. v. Kent at Lord's, but it was not until nearly another year had passed that he reached the magic figures again with 139 for the M.C.C. against Cambridge University at Fenner's; while a month later at Lord's the Champion took a further 196 runs off the Cantab bowling, recording his highest score on that ground. Apart from " W.G.'s " big score, this match at Lord's was notable for a long stand between " W.G." and " W.G., Junior"; the only occasion, as far as I can trace, when the two " W.G.s " were masters of the bowling. They played on the same side many times; once at Ashley Down on an August Bank Holiday, and how we hoped, when they went out to open the innings together, that we should see father and son give the side a good start. But it was not to be; the son made only 1, the father 301. The younger " W.G." looked more of the student than the athlete. I used to watch him at Clifton College matches and at the College sports, but to me this tall, bespectacled young man always seemed to be out of his element. Quiet, reserved, shy and unemotional, he was entirely different from other members of the Grace family I had the privilege of meeting at one time or another, and despite intensive training as a lad and the best of coaching in later years, he failed to overcome a natural awkwardness of pose and style as a batsman. He gained his place in the Clifton College XI, however, and proved that it was not the result of the famous name he bore, by having in his last year a batting average of 29 and a bowling record of 51 wickets for 11 runs each. From Clifton he went to Cambridge and delighted his father by a fine start in the Freshmen's match, but his form did not apparently impress his captain and his prospects of getting a " Blue " seemed remote. In 1895, however, " W.G.'s " great year, young " W.G." got his place in the Cambridge XI against Oxford, and justified it with scores of 40 and 28, taking part in a useful opening stand with Frank Mitchell, the brilliant Yorkshireman. The following year saw " W.G., Junior," again in the Cambridge team at Lord's, but he was dismimssed without scoring in each innings. What his father's feelings were on that occasion can be imagined, but not expressed. For Gloucestershire young " W.G." was singularly unfortunate, failing to produce either batting or bowling form to suggest he was up to county standard, except on a few occasions, during the five seasons when he played occasionally for the team.

CHAPTER XV

The opening of the season of 1895 found " W.G." more optimistic than for some time past, one reason being that the trouble in his leg, which had handicapped him during the previous two summers, had entirely disappeared, and also because he looked forward to having a much stronger XI than had hitherto been possible. The spring was genial and he was able to get plenty of practice. At the nets every morning he was as fit as a man nearing his 48th birthday could be, for his opening match of the season, the M.C.C. v. Sussex, at Lord's. This game, played in the second week of May, gave the Champion his 99th century. In the first innings he was out to a brilliant catch by K. S. Ranjitsinhji, who was making his first appearance for Sussex, but in the second he was not dismissed until he had made 103, when " Ranji " again secured his wicket. For some unexplained reason " W.G." did very little bowling in this match, probably because he feared a return of his leg trouble, but when he did go on in the Sussex second innings, he bowled the young Indian Prince, who had scored 150, with his first ball. This was " Ranji's " first experience of the Doctor's simple-looking bowling, and he must have been very surprised when the ball passed his bat and broke the wicket.

" W.G.'s " next game was for Gloucestershire against Somerset, who had become a first-class county only as recently as 1891, and against whom the Doctor had fared somewhat indifferently. In consequence there was a disheartening attendance at the County Ground, Bristol, when this historic game opened. Somerset won the toss and commenced batting, L. C. H. Palairet and G. Fowler taking the score past 200 before the first wicket fell; and how the game was viewed by Somerset during this long partnership has been told by " Sammy " Woods, as related by my old friend, F. C. Bracher, who must be very proud to recall that he had the privilege of taking part in so memorable a game. Indeed, all who survive must look back with pride on this game which was to figure so prominently in the annals of cricket. Sam Woods has gone, and so has that good soldier-cricketer, H. T. Stanley, killed in the South African War, while others who are no longer with us are Board, Murch, Tyler, Painter and Johnny Ferris. But those who remain will never forget the cricket which followed the close of Somerset's first innings, which, thanks to some good bowling by " W.G.," only totalled 303. " W.G.," as was his custom that season, took Johnny Ferris in with him, but the latter was bowled for 4, while C. O. H. Sewell, playing in his first match for Gloucestershire, was caught and bowled by Sam Woods for 2. Two wickets down for 15, and the odds on Somerset, that was the position when a tall, slim youth came down the Pavilion steps—C. L. Townsend, still in his teens, shy and reserved and at this stage of his career very nervous, naturally, for his previous best score for the county had been but 17. The faith that inspired the " Old Man " to put this Clifton College boy in so early was fully justified, for Charles Townsend played an inspired innings that day, and we saw the oldest and youngest of first-class cricketers meeting the fastest that Sam Woods could send down and the most puzzling of Tyler's spinning slows with supreme confidence and skill. " W.G." was nearing his century of centuries, and the crowd—if such a term could be applied to so small a company of spectators—followed each stroke with bated breath, while the Champion played on, cool, confident and completely master of the situation. As his score approached the magic number, Sam Woods, who was bowling, turned round and looked at the score box; one of the scorers leant out and held up two fingers. Sam ran slowly up to the wicket and delivered a full toss on the leg side, and the Master, getting the ball in the middle of the bat, despatched it to the boundary. This stroke made history. The great " W.G." had achieved his ambition; he had completed his hundredth hundred! There was a wild outburst of cheering. Everyone who had seats rose. Hats and caps were waved in the air, and all the Somerset team joined in the applause, while the black-bearded hero turned to each side of the ground and raised the peak of his M.C.C. cap. In the pavilion was his brother, " E.M.," who would have given much to have been in young Townsend's place on this supreme occasion; while in the enclosure, flushed with excitement but overjoyed in her own quiet way, was Mrs. Grace with her daughter.

There was another outburst of enthusiasm when " W.G." with an off-drive to the boundary passed the second hundred, and while the spectators were still cheering, a magnum of champagne was brought out on a tray. " W.G." only drank champagne on special occasions, but was there ever a more special occasion that this? C. L. Townsend looked to be set for a hundred, too, but when only five short was out leg before. Jack Painter and F. C. Bracher were the only other members of the team to give the Doctor any assistance, and at last his great innings was closed by a catch by Tyler off Sam Woods. He had batted for $5\frac{1}{2}$ hours without giving a chance and without making a false stroke or getting a run that was not played for, and all who could remember the " W.G." of the 70's agreed that he had never compiled a big score by playing more perfect cricket. " His cuts," stated a local newspaper, " square and late, were perfect, the ball travelling over the close cut turf and reaching the boundary before the most agile of fielders had a chance to intervene; his drives were vigorous and safe and his fours followed fast upon each other. The spectators were worked into a stage of great enthusiasm which warmed their hearts while their fingers were half frozen by the biting wind." It will be recalled that the day, which opened bright and sunny, turned very cold later, and actually while the Master's innings was in progress his big beard was decorated by snow flakes. He scored at the rate of 55 runs an hour, and hit no fewer than 38 fours. In one of the London newspapers regret was expressed that he had not been able to delay his triumph and achieve it at Lord's, but long afterwards I heard the Doctor express his satisfaction that the great event took place in his own county and on the ground in which he had such deep personal interest, and where he had not before scored a century. The Gloucestershire innings realised 474; Somerset in their second innings could only muster 189, and the home county won by nine wickets, their first victory over Somerset as a first-class county. Here are the full scores of this memorable match:—

SOMERSET

L. C. H. PALAIRET, c Bracher, b Roberts	80	c Board, b Murch	1
G. FOWLER, st Board, b W. G. Grace ..	118	lbw, b Townsend	33
J. B. CHALLEN, b W. G. Grace	6	c Wrathall, b Townsend	16
R. C. N. PALAIRET, c Board, b Murch ..	26	c Roberts, b Murch	23
H. T. STANLEY, c Board, b Murch	29	b Murch	31
S. M. J. WOODS, c Board, b Murch	6	c Painter, b Murch	47
D. L. EVANS, lbw, b W. G. Grace	11	c Board, b Murch	2
NICHOLLS, c Board, b W. G. Grace	0	c Board, b Murch	6
TYLER, c Ferris, b W. G. Grace	0	not out	17

Rev. A. P. WICKHAM, c Thomas, b Murch	3	b Murch	0
BUCKNELL, not out	10	b Murch	0
Extras	14	Extras	13
	303		**189**

GLOUCESTERSHIRE

W. G. GRACE, c Tyler, b Woods	288		
J. J. FERRIS, b Tyler	4		
C. O. H. SEWELL, c and b Woods	2		
C. L. TOWNSEND, lbw, b Bucknell	95		
PAINTER, lbw, b Tyler	34		
WRATHALL, b Fowler	6	not out	6
E. L. THOMAS, b Woods	3	lbw, b Bucknell	12
F. C. BRACHER, b Bucknell	20		
MURCH, c Stanley, b Tyler	5		
BOARD, not out	2	not out	1
ROBERTS, c Sub., b Tyler	9		
Extras	6		
	474		**19**

BOWLING

SOMERSETSHIRE.	1st inns.	Murch 4—72.	W. G. Grace 5—87. Roberts 1—51.
	2nd inns.	Murch 8—68.	C. L. Townsend 2—63.
GLOUCESTERSHIRE.	1st inns.	Tyler 4 —160.	Woods 2—145. Bucknell 2—68.
	2nd inns.	Fowler 1—5.	

RESULT—GLOUCESTERSHIRE won by 9 wickets.

If one man more than another in a cricket match is in a position to judge the merits of a batting performance, it is the wicket-keeper, for he is right on the spot and gets a close-up view of every shot; his nose is sometimes within a few inches of the bat, and nothing good or bad, lucky or unlucky, escapes his keen vision. In the game in which " W.G." scored his century of centuries, Prebendary A. P. Wickham was Somerset's wicket-keeper and he has been good enough to give his recollection of this famous occasion. Here are his own words:—

" The remarkable thing about W. G. Grace's innings was that he only allowed four balls to pass him. He was batting for more than five and a half hours, and I had quite an easy time watching him. It did not matter what the bowling was like—he never let the ball alone, but got it somehow. If they bowled at his beard he would put it away to leg. Tyler tried pitching some of his deliveries outside the off-stump, but " W.G." would drive it one way or another. It was a wonderful innings. There was an interesting sequel. I told the story once to C. J. Robinson, an old Somerset cricketer, and he passed it on to Hobbs and Strudwick and they said they could not believe it. Some time afterwards I met Hobbs and Strudwick and told them myself. They said they believed it then. After that Mr. Robinson went to see the first match at the Oval. Surrey played Kent. Hobbs went to the wicket and allowed five balls in the first over to go past him. What I have in mind about that incident is that Hobbs let more balls alone in one over than " W.G." did in 5½ hours."

This authoritative statement about " W.G." allowing only four balls to pass his bat in 5½ hours is much appreciated. Had it not been placed on record by the one man whose word cannot be doubted, nobody would have believed it possible. The score-card, however, corroborates in a measure Prebendary Wickham's statement, for there were only 4 byes in the total of 474.

A few days after defeating Somerset, Gloucestershire went down to Gravesend to play Kent. The ground is a small one with, if my memory serves me, a slope from one end. The pitch on this day in the third week in May, 1895, was as perfect as could be, and " W.G." must have given his beard an extra pull when F. W. Marchant beat him for the choice of innings, for rarely had Gloucestershire taken the field with a less impressive array of bowlers. There was Fred Roberts, it is true, but for the other end " W.G." only had Bill Murch —who had taken only 10 wickets during the previous season, although he had bowled well against Somerset at Bristol— and himself. No one else in the team was a recognised bowler, but before the Kent innings closed three players, C. O. H. Sewell, S. A. P. Kitcat, and C. J. Francis who had never before bowled in a county match, bowled for the first and only time in their careers. Kent scored 470—a score which should have made them safe from defeat—but they had yet to reckon with the Doctor, who, going in first with Harry Wrathall, saw all the rest come and go save Fred Roberts, while he scored 257. He took 7½ hours over the runs, and it was said in the Press that he gave a chance at 80, but Jack Painter, who was in with him, assured me that he did not and that the critics were wrong. So here is something about " W.G.'s " batting in the first two county games of 1895 that has been overlooked; he batted 13 hours, scored 545 runs, and gave no chance. Gloucestershire scored 443, the innings closing at lunch time on the third day. What were the odds on the

match being finished when in one innings each the two teams
had totalled 913 runs? A seasoned gambler would probably
have laid 1,000—1, especially if he were competent to judge
the state of the pitch, yet a quarter of an hour before stumps
were due to be drawn the game was over, and Gloucestershire
had won by nine wickets. The extraordinary climax to this
game was due to a chance which compelled " W.G." to put
Jack Painter on to open bowling with Fred Roberts. It has
been said that the Doctor did not mean Jack Painter to bowl;
that he intended Murch to start, but the ball, as he tossed it,
slipped out of his hand and went towards Painter who, picking
it up, proceeded to mark out his bowling run. This, however, is not true, for Murch was not on the field; for travelling
to Gravesend on the first day, he missed the train and did not
arrive on the ground until 5.30, while on the second day he
left to fulfil a match engagement in Wiltshire. Unless
" W.G." put himself on, there was only Painter, who went on
and accomplished an amazing piece of bowling; for getting
a good c and b in his first over, he proceeded to go right
through the Kent XI, dismissing seven batsmen on a wicket
that was wearing remarkably well. In Kent's first innings he
had been put on last and had bowled only half-a-dozen overs,
while during the previous season he had not bowled at all,
and was not even regarded as a change bowler. Kent were
all out for 76, and Gloucestershire were left to get 103 in 75
minutes, a task which they accomplished with nearly a quarter
of an hour to spare, thanks to the Champion who was 73 not
out at the finish. " W.G." had made so many records in his
time that it seemed impossible, at his age, to add to them,
but at Gravesend he had an absolutely unique experience,
being on the field from the opening to the close of the match.
He fielded the first ball sent down by Roberts; he made the
winning hit off the last ball, and was either batting, bowling or
fielding every other moment of the game, as he was last man
out in Gloucestershire's first innings. This sensational finish
created interest everywhere, and when the Gloucestershire XI
arrived at Bristol station at midnight, there was a large crowd
waiting to give " W.G." and Painter a rousing welcome. This,
by the way, is the only known occasion on which Gloucestershire cricketers have been welcomed home after a victory, and
needless to say, " W.G." was very pleased at this reception.

After a few days rest the Champion was in the field again
at the Oval, playing in W. W. Read's testimonial match, and

it was not the great left-hander who drew the crowds, but
the Doctor who, between May 9th and 25th had scored 829
runs. The great crowd who gathered at the Oval to see
" W.G." add to this grand total were, however, disappointed,
for he was bowled by Tom Richardson for 18; and any chance
he might have had to reach his 1,000 runs in that match was
thwarted by the collapse of Surrey in their second innings,
making it unnecessary for England to bat again. Only one
more chance remained—the Gloucestershire v. Middlesex
match at Lord's, which was due to commence on May 30th;
and the Doctor required no less than 153 runs to bring his
total to the coveted four figures. Fortune was with him,
and on winning the toss he opened the innings with Wrathall,
and although he had to face a varied attack which included
J. T. Hearne, then at his best, Rawlin and E. A. Nepean,
who delivered an exceedingly puzzling sample of slow spinner,
" W.G." started with complete confidence; but he was, on the
whole, more subdued than usual, scoring only 58 runs between
noon and the luncheon interval, which in those days was taken
at 2 p.m. After lunch, however, the Champion threw caution
to the winds and set about the bowling with all his old
dominating command of timing, placing and driving, and
when he had advanced his score to 99 there was a " breath-
less hush " as the next ball was delivered. " W.G.," as easy
in mind as a fisherman waiting for a bite, coolly placed the
ball on the leg side and jogged down the pitch to the accom-
paniment of an enthusiasm that indicated how great a relief
it was to the spectators. Another 53 runs, however, had to
be scored and Gloucestershire were none too strong in batting; but A. J. Dearlove, a Bristol player, whose steady
defence had helped the county out of trouble on more than
one occasion, remained while his captain went on with his
task; and at last, with his score at 149, Nepean sent down a
long hop on the leg side which the Doctor hit to the boundary,
and the feat had been accomplished. Here on the very ground
where in 1868 he had scored his first century for the Gentlemen against the Players, " W.G." had now registered his
thousand runs in May, and at nearly 48 years of age. Such
was the enthusiasm of the crowd that it was some minutes
before the game could continue, but when it did " W.G." went
on to score 169 and then returned, smiling with satisfaction,
to the Pavilion.

Here is the Doctor's record from May 9th to May 30th, 1895:—

M.C.C. v. Sussex	13 and 103	116
M.C.C. v. Yorkshire	18 and 25	43
Gloucestershire v. Somerset ...		288
A. J. Webbe's XI v. Cambridge Un.		52
Gloucestershire v. Kent	257 and 73 not	330
England v. Surrey		18
Gloucestershire v. Middlesex ...		169
	Total	**1,016**

" W.G." did not return to Bristol after his historic game but went on to Brighton where he just missed another century by 9 runs. Had he returned to his native city he would undoubtedly have found thousands of his supporters waiting to acclaim his unprecedented feat. After his innings at Brighton, rain-affected wickets caused him to have a moderate spell and it was not until after the beginning of August that he returned to his best form with a score of 119 against Notts at Cheltenham. At Lord's, for the Gentlemen, he and A. E. Stoddart put on 151 for the first wicket before the latter was out, but " W.G." went on to score 118 out of 241 before he was dismissed. With an aggregate of 2,346 runs, including nine centuries, he was third in the first class averages (51), a grand effort for a man of his years.

Gloucestershire, thanks to " W.G.'s " batting, and the bowling of C. L. Townsend, who took over 100 wickets, were fourth in the Championship, winning 8 games and losing 6, but as " E.M." had now dropped out of county cricket, " W.G." was the only survivor of the old brigade.

In November, 1895, Henry, the eldest of the brotherhood, died from apoplexy at the age of 62; though never coming prominently before the public like his younger brothers, Henry was, in his younger days, an excellent cricketer and but for the calls of his profession might quite well have made a name for himself in important games. Described as a vigorous bat, a medium pace round-arm bowler and an excellent fielder, he made 63 not out on his first appearance at Lord's in 1861, an innings which helped the South Wales Club to beat the M.C.C. by 7 wickets.

Before passing on to 1896 it may interest readers to learn the reactions of the British sporting public to W. G. Grace's feat of scoring 1,000 runs in May. Throughout the country swept the wave of " W.G." worship; newspapers everywhere referred in glowing terms to the greatest cricketer of all time, while one announced that practical recognition had already come from an unexpected source, the Balloon Society of Great Britain, who had passed the following resolution:—

> " That the gold medal of the Society be awarded to W. G. Grace, Esq., M.D., in recognition of his prominence in all open-air sports, and our national game of cricket, all of which tend so efficiently to the healthy development and preservation of the characteristics of active Englishmen."

Many and varied were the tributes paid by the press to the national hero with a practical effect on the various testimonial funds, and it was no wonder that the response was magnificent and worthy of the deeds that had prompted them. The amount raised by the " Daily Telegraph " was £2,377 2s. 6d., and by the Committee of Gloucestershire, of which the Duke of Beaufort was president, £1,436 3s. 8d., making a total for Dr. Grace of £9,073 8s. 3d. The feeling of every subscriber was beautifully expressed by Sir Edward Lawson, afterwards Lord Burnham, in forwarding to Dr. Grace the " Daily Telegraph's " cheque:—

> " Such a magnificent demonstration is due, sir, in the first place to a warm appreciation felt throughout the land and the Empire for your own high and worthy qualities as an English cricketer. It comprises, however, beyond this, a very notable and emphatic expression of the general love for these out-door sports and pursuits which, free from any element of cruelty, greed or coarseness, most and best develop our British traits of manliness, healthy training of the mind and body; and at the same time giving pleasure and amusement to the greatest possible number.
>
> " In this respect I permit myself to regard the progress and result of the ' National Shilling Testimonial ' as a manifestation by classes and masses alike of their abiding preference for wholesome and honest amusements in contradistinction to sickly pleasures and puritanical gloom, thus conferring upon you, sir, the happy distinc-

tion of a substantial personal tribute, which is, at the
same time a public approval of your salutary example to
the youth and manhood of our time."

It is strange that beyond a brief statement that £100 had
been voted by the Gloucestershire Committee to the W. G.
Grace Testimonial Fund there is nothing in the club's records
to indicate official satisfaction at the wonderful doings of the
Gloucestershire captain. There is no resolution of congratu-
lation, no expression from any member of the Committee,
when they met just after " W.G." had blazed a trail of triumph
across the playing fields of England, and even the banquet
which was held at the Victoria Rooms, Clifton, on June 24th
—the " Century of Centuries Banquet," as it was called—had
no mention in the Minutes of the Committee until July 1st,
when it was resolved

" That the thanks of the Committee be given to Mr.
J. W. Arrowsmith for the admirable manner he arranged
and managed the W. G. Grace banquet, and they con-
gratulate him that so great an undertaking should have
gone off so successfully and without the slightest hitch."

At the same meeting the Committee of the Gloucestershire
Club also congratulated the Duke and Duchess of Beaufort
on the attainment of their Golden Wedding, an incident, by
the by, which recalls a pleasant visit to Badminton and an
opportunity to drink with many others the health of this grand
old sportsman and his Duchess from the Loving Cup passed
round. The omission of any allusion to the greatest hero of
sport England has ever known and his wonderful achievements
in May, 1895, is strange and can only be accounted for by
the fact that the Secretary, the record-keeper, was " W.G.'s "
brother who had a natural disinclination to extol the deeds
of a member of his family. The fact, however, remains that
if the story of " W.G.'s " life were written from the records of
the County Club it would be a very meagre one, confined
largely to such facts as the drawing of the princely sum of £36
to pay his assistant while he played cricket for the county.
Among the many tributes paid to " W.G." in 1895, the one
which he prized the most was that received from the Prince
of Wales. Everyone was delighted with the expression of
appreciation by His Royal Highness, and the general view
was expressed by the " Pall Mall Gazette " in the following
terms:—

"We suppose that this is the first time the compliment has been paid to a cricketer. We are grateful to the Prince for his official recognition that the performances of Dr. W. G. Grace are as important and as worthy of such great public recognition as any of the more solemn performances for which royal letters are generally received.

"Of Dr. Grace we say nothing. He has drained the language of eulogy and it is no use applying superlatives to him any more. Perhaps the highest testimonial of all to his powers is the fact that at this moment Gloucestershire—Gloucestershire!—stands at the top of all the first class counties."

The writer of this interesting editorial note might have added that not only was Gloucestershire at the top of the table, but when the averages were published on June 4th, a Gloucestershire man—" W.G.," of course—was head of the batting, while another, Jack Painter, topped the bowling averages.

During the height of the enthusiasm over " W.G.'s " wonderful deeds on the cricket field one of the London newspapers suggested that he should be knighted: a " man like W. G. Grace," it declared, " the embodiment of muscle, courage and nerve, is a national glory. Now is the time for the Government to recognise this by meeting the universal desire of millions who scan his scores day by day, that a distinction should be placed upon cricket and cricketers in his name. No act more satisfactory to Englishmen could be performed at this moment than a knighthood for W. G. Grace. Let the Government go to the country on it and it may be predicted with absolute certainty that any candidate who objected to the honour being conferred would lose his seat."

" Punch " suggested that the new title should be " Dr. Grace, C.B. (Companion of the Bat) " and added:—

"Another title! Supplemental gazette of the Birthday Honours, Dr. W. G. Grace to be Cricket Field-Marshal."

Henry Labouchere in " Truth " emphasised the eagerness for news of " W.G.'s " scores by the following story of Jabez Balfour, who was then undergoing his trial at Bow Street Police Court:—

" . . . I mentioned the other week that Balfour had shown remarkable coolness in the dock. A good story reaches me in illustration of his behaviour. It was one of the days when Mr. Grace was running up centuries and even in the Extradition Court the score was being followed with great interest. The reporter of an evening paper had a seat so close to the dock that Balfour, by stretching slightly, could peruse some portions of the paper, copies of each edition being sent up to its representative. Balfour was seen to be making furtive attempts to read something but whether his own trial or the cricket report was not certain until eventually discovered in the attempt, he said in a stage-whisper, ' How many did Grace make?' When he had recovered his presence of mind, the journalist whispered back the score and received a grateful look."

" Truth " also had this to say on the suggested knighthood:—

" As to the chief exponent of the national game, it would be a most graceful and popular act were Mr. Grace to be knighted by the Sovereign. Far better does he deserve the distinction than do those hangers-on of the official world who earn it by hours of obsequious begging in the office of a Ministerial Secretary."

CHAPTER XVI

When the season of 1896 opened the county's prospects were much brighter than they had been for years; new stars had arisen and the " Grand Old Man " would no longer have to play almost a lone hand in the fortunes of the club, and if it had not been for the skeleton in the cupboard he would indeed have been a happy warrior with such a band of brilliant young men around him as Charles Townsend, Gilbert Jessop, R. W. Rice, F. H. B. Champain, W. S. A. Brown and others. This was a golden era for the game of cricket; nearly every county had young players whose names are inscribed on the scroll of cricket fame, but the Champion of the '60's remained the Champion of the '90's. His batting feats were less dramatic than in 1895, but during the season he built up the huge total of 2,135 runs, and for 54 innings in first-class cricket had an average of 42. This would have been an outstanding record for a player in the heyday of early manhood, but " W.G." was competing now against players who had been either babies or unborn when he was making hundreds in first-class cricket. He opened the season well, scoring 108 against the Colts on the County Ground, Bristol. A century with twenty-two active young cricketers in the field, each trying to outdo the other in saving runs, is no mean achievement, but it was a mild curtain-raiser to a great performance which set the cricket world ringing with praise for the so-called veteran before the season was over. It was Gloucestershire's custom for many years to play Sussex at Brighton on Whit-Monday and the following days. " W.G." was very partial to this ground, and has recorded his opinion that it was one of the easiest scoring grounds in the country.

On this occasion winning the toss, he started batting with Harry Wrathall, and a very good start, too, for the score was nearly one hundred before Wrathall left. " The Old Man," however, played on; he saw all the young men come and go, and when the innings concluded for a total of 463, " W.G.'s " contribution was a magnificent 243 not out. When the teams met again that year it was on August Bank Holiday; a really beautiful day—one of the few really perfect days we have ever had for the Bank Holiday match at Bristol. John Spry had the ground in glorious trim—and no ground in the whole country responded better to skilled and persistent attention when weather conditions lent a hand than the stretch of turf at Ashley Down. The prospect of seeing " W.G." and Prince Ranjitsinhji, the two most popular personalities in the game, caused the spectators to pour on to the ground in thousands, and when the two captains came out to toss for choice of innings, everybody awaited the result. " W.G.'s " luck was in at the start; he won the toss and took his son in with him to open the innings. Unfortunately, before play had been in progress many minutes, young " W.G." was back in the pavilion, bowled for 1, and one can easily imagine the disappointment of his father. This, however, was the only wicket Sussex obtained until late in the day for R. W. Rice joined the Doctor and they obtained a mastery over the bowling. The early disappointment was forgotten in the feast of batting which followed—R. W. Rice as steady as a rock, playing all the bowling brought into action like the proverbial book, and occasionally, when it was perfectly safe, hitting one to the long on boundary; while " W.G." was his old brilliant self, cool, confident and especially effective with his scoring strokes to all parts of the field. At the end of the day he was still there; his score was 195 and the total 341. What a scene there was when the umpires took the bails off and the players left the field! Spectators broke the lines and came charging across the turf, eager to get to the " Old Man " and show him their delight, but John Spry and his assistants did the distance to the wicket with stakes and ropes to protect the pitch in record time and when " W.G." had succeeded in struggling through the wildly excited crowd and had reached the pavilion, a dense throng remained cheering until he came to a window and waved in answer to their clamour. The next day "W.G." went on batting until all the wickets but one had fallen, and with his score at 301 he was bowled by A. C. Collins, and the third best innings of his career was over. Batting eight and a half hours without a chance, his huge score was made up of 29 fours, 16 threes, 27 twos and 83 singles. Gloucestershire's total was 551, and Sussex had to acknowledge defeat by an innings and 123 runs. Incidentally, in two innings against Sussex Dr. Grace had scored 544 runs for once out. Later on in the season he made 102 not out against Lancashire at Bristol, and 186 against Somerset at Taunton.

Apart from " W.G.'s " wonderful batting the outstanding event of Gloucestershire's cricket in 1896 was their memorable game with the Australians at Cheltenham, when they were put out for a mere 17 runs. The County XI on this occasion was: W. G. Grace, R. W. Rice, W. M. Hemingway, C. O. H. Sewell, G. L. Jessop, C. L. Townsend, W. G. Grace Junior, F. H. B. Champain, W. S. A. Brown, Wrathall and Board. A combination of rain and sunshine had produced a surface so treacherous that nine batsmen were dismissed for 6 runs, while " W.G." was top scorer with 9, and there were two byes. The bowlers responsible for the county's record low score were Hugh Trumble who took 6 wickets for 8, and T. R. McKibbin with 4 for 7. The unexpected happened in this match with a vengeance, and those who took part in it will probably agree that one such experience is sufficient in a life time.

It was during 1896 that the cricket world was startled by a strike of professionals who had been selected to play for England versus Australia at the Oval, their grievance being that the amount they received for the game was inadequate, and in the controversy which followed much was said and written about the large sums certain amateurs received as expenses. So pointed were some of the remarks that the Surrey County Committee were constrained to issue the following official statement:—

> " The Committee of the Surrey County Cricket Club have observed paragraphs in the press respecting amounts alleged to be paid or promised to Dr. W. G. Grace for playing in the match, England v. Australia. The Committee desire to give the statements contained in the paragraphs the most unqualified contradiction. During many years, on the occasions of Dr. W. G. Grace playing at the Oval, at the request of the Surrey Committee, in the matches Gentlemen v. Players and England v. Australia, Dr. Grace has received the sum of £10 a match to cover his expenses in coming to and remaining in London during the three days. Beyond this amount Dr. Grace has not received, directly or indirectly, one farthing for playing in a match at the Oval.—Signed on behalf of the Committee, C. W. Alcock, August 10, 1896.

This official statement at once checked the absurd discussion about what the Champion was receiving, and it was doubtful whether £10 actually covered travelling, hotel and other costs incurred by Dr. Grace for such an occasion as a Test Match in London. The professionals then climbed down and the matter was at an end, but it had served to lay, once and for all, the ghost concerning the small fortune that " W.G." was supposed to making out of cricket.

It was in 1896, too, that " E.M.'s " long period of " active service in the field " came to an end; he played against the Australians in June, scoring 7 and 1, and taking 2 wickets for 45, and against Warwickshire in July, when he did better than some of the younger players, even though his batting produced only 11 and 9 and his bowling 1 for 18. This was " E.M.'s " last game for Gloucestershire, and no other player of the game, except " W.G.," could match the period over which his career in important cricket extended, for he played for West Gloucestershire against All-England in 1855 (when less than 14 years of age) and was 55 when his final appearance in the Gloucestershire XI concluded his career. It was not, of course, known, when Warwickshire had won the game and the players had left the field that we should never again see the old Coroner taking part in a match at Ashley Down or there would surely have been a desire on the part of the spectators to pay tribute to this fine old veteran for his long service for the county club, service that can never be appraised by his statistical record. It was given without stint of personal effort, and with nothing in the shape of reward to which the word " remuneration " can be applied. " E.M." had no office staff to do the vast amount of clerical work in his office as secretary, which, of course, he carried on for some years after he had ceased playing; there was no shorthand writer or typist and he did all the work himself with an amount of care and attention to detail that was astonishing. Mr. R. E. Bush, who knew him as well as anyone in the county, told me that when a county game was in progress at Ashley Down early in the season, " E.M." would be stopped a dozen times in walking through the enclosure by people wanting to pay their sub-scriptions, and he would take their money, put it in his capacious pockets, make a joking remark, and pass on. He never made a memorandum of the amounts he received, or a note to remind him of the numbers who paid, yet without fail the receipt and ticket would arrive the next morning.

" E.M.'s " batting and bowling figures for the county bear no comparison to those of his brother, " W.G.," in fact, only four centuries stand to his credit and only 40 other scores of over fifty; but his value to the side cannot be judged by scores and averages. Who can estimate the value of his uncanny skill and nerve as a fielder at point? All the best judges agree that there has never been his equal for snapping up half chances, for " E.M." didn't mind how they came along as long as they did come, and many a batsman got himself out trying to hit a hole through the daring fielder, who was near enough almost to smell the varnish on the bat. The story of the swallow was originally associated with the " little Doctor." You remember it, of course? An attempt to take a quick one at point, and catching a swallow instead of the ball. It has been tacked on to various cricketers, but was first told to emphasise " E.M.'s " quickness of hand and eye in the one place in the field where a man had to be quick or he would be liable to get hurt.

Dr. E. M. Grace is now only a memory, but what a memory! Looking back over the years I can recall scores of kindnesses received at his hand—lifts in his buggy along country roads, help and consideration on a great many occasions in work-a-day life and happy hours in the cricket field. When he gave up the office of secretary to the County Club in 1909, after nearly forty years' service, it was a great satisfaction to be asked to assist as one of the secretaries to his testimonial fund, and I recall posting hundreds of invitations to subscribe, the result being a sum of £600 which, with a serviceable walking-stick, was presented to Dr. E. M. by the Duke of Beaufort at the Grand Hotel, Bristol, at the end of the season. " E.M." carried on in club cricket for many years, and at the age of 63 put the young men to shame by playing right through two innings in succession for Thornbury. He died on May 20th, 1911, at the age of 69, and was buried at Downend, his old home; and those who were present at that service will never forget the sadness of the occasion, and the singing of " E.M.'s " favourite hymn, " Tell me the old, old story."

In 1897, although failing to keep up his wonderful form of the two previous seasons, " W.G." scored over 1,500 runs for an average of just under 40, and had the satisfaction of seeing Gloucestershire rise from 10th to 5th place in the Championship. His total of hundreds increased by four (all compiled for his county), two being at the expense of Notts, while against the Philadelphians at Bristol both he and Jessop made over a century, " W.G." also taking seven wickets for 91. The following year, which was to prove his last for Gloucestershire, saw him attain his 50th birthday, an occasion which brought forth yet another outburst of popular enthusiasm, and he received tributes which, as far as I know, have been accorded to no other Englishman outside royalty. During this season he scored three more centuries, but they were all made on opponents' grounds, his highest effort at home being 93 not out against Sussex at the County Ground, Bristol, an innings that is a curiosity in cricket for it is the only instance on record of a batsman deliberately declining the opportunity of making a hundred. Eight wickets had fallen in the second innings, and there was no chance whatever of the game being finished, and at the other end the batsman, W. S. A. Brown, was well set. A large August Bank Holiday crowd was preparing to give the " Old Man " a cheer when he completed his hundred, but they were doomed to disappointment for when 7 short of the coveted number, and with only half an hour left to play, " W.G." declared and the players left the field. To the majority of those present such a declaration was inexplicable: there seemed no reason for it, but there was. " W.G." had, during his long career, made every score from 0 to 100, except 93, and it was to complete the record that he declared when he had reached that score.

This was Dr. Grace's last regular season with Gloucestershire, and it is a happy thought that he was able to lead, during the last two months of 1898, a side that had few superiors in the whole country, but trouble came thick and fast upon the shoulders of the Grand Old Man after this notable season had passed. At the end of the year his daughter, Miss Bessie Grace, passed away, and early in the following season the difference, which had been brewing so long behind the scenes, came to a head. It will be recalled that the season of 1899 opened as usual with the Colts match at Ashley Down, and a very interesting trial it was, for two of the Colts, F. G. Robinson and P. G. Robinson, some years later captained the County XI, while another was L. D. Brownlee, as brilliant a batsman as any in the country when he was careful enough to get set, and an outfielder without a superior. " W.G." did not play, and W. Troup, who had been appointed Vice-Captain, took charge of the county side.

However, Dr. Grace went on the Southern Tour, which opened the season, but as soon as the four games against Sussex, Kent, Surrey and Middlesex were over he received a copy of the resolution passed by the Committee on May 16th. This resolution, which was the direct cause of " W.G." severing his connection with Gloucestershire, was as follows:—

> " That the Secretary write to Dr. W. G. Grace immediately the tour is over, asking him from the Committee to state exactly what matches he intends playing in for the county during this year."

One gathers that some member of the Committee had heard that Dr. W. G. Grace had received an invitation to become manager of the new cricket ground at the Crystal Palace, and also captain of the London County Club then being formed. It is very difficult indeed after so much time, and without a full knowledge of the facts, to form a just opinion of the wisdom of presenting something of an ultimatum to such a man as " W.G.," but it must have been known to the Committee that it would be resented, and would lead to the Doctor deciding to take on this new job if he had not already made up his mind to do so. And was it really necessary that a break should be forced in this way? Surely the Committee must have been aware of the famous cricketer's devotion to the interests of his county, and that he would rather sacrifice his own well-being than do anything that would injure the Gloucestershire Club. These are thoughts that arise in contemplating this drastic resolution. Whatever else " W.G." might have been, he was never selfish or mercenary, and it must have been known to the Committee that his temperament would never suffer interference in a dictatorial spirit. Regarding the sad episode from the evidence of the Minute Book, one is forced to the conclusion that there was a lamentable lack of tact on the Committee's part in handling the situation. The resolution, in the circumstances, was unnecessary; Dr. Grace was still in command of the XI; he had played in each game so far, and any action on the part of the Committee should have been delayed until they had reason to complain of absence from matches or inattention to the interests of the club. Dr. Grace's reply to this resolution showed plainly and unmistakably that he resented the action of his colleagues; his letter has been preserved and is the only document in his familiar handwriting that appears in the records of the Gloucestershire Club.

St. Andrew's,

Lawrie Park Road,

Sydenham, S.E.

May 28th, 1899.

To the Committee of the Gloucestershire County Club.

Gentlemen, in answer to yours of the 26th, re resolution passed on the 16th and kept back from me for reasons best known to yourselves, I beg to state that I had intended to play in nearly all our matches, but in consequence of the resolution passed and other actions of some of the Committee, I send in my resignation as captain, and must ask the Committee to choose the teams for future games, as I shall not get them up.

I have always tried my very best to promote the interests of the Gloucestershire County Club, and it is with deep regret that I resign the captaincy. I have the greatest affection for the county of my birth, but for the Committee as a body, the greatest contempt.

I am,

Yours truly,

W. G. GRACE.

Except for the sting in the tail of this letter, the reply is unlike the characteristic expression of " W.G." when he considered he had been affronted, and it looks as if the old warrior had tried very hard to repress his wrath and until he came to the end had been very successful, but the last few words were severe, and one cannot but regret that they were included.

The effect of this letter is indicated by the entries in the Minute Book, dated June 2nd, 1899.

" A letter dated May 28th was read from Dr. W. G. Grace to the chairman as such, in reply to the resolution passed at the last Committee meeting, in which expression was used to the effect that he (the writer) held the Committee in the greatest contempt.

" RESOLVED: That the Committee is of opinion that no self-respecting body could accept such terms, and that in the hope that Dr. W. G. Grace would, on reflection, see his way clear to withdrawing them, this meeting stands adjourned."

Dr. Grace did not see his way to withdrawing his remark; he stood by his guns; and the Committee stood by theirs, and at their next meeting passed the following resolution:

"That while the Committee are conscious of the great services rendered by Dr. W. G. Grace to the Gloucestershire County Cricket Club as well as to cricket generally, and feel deep regret at his severance from them in spite of the efforts which have been made by them to avoid it, they feel they have no course open to them but to accept his resignation."

In this regrettable way, the greatest of all cricketers passed out of active association with the Gloucestershire County Club. It was all very sad, and one might add, unnecessary, for in the natural course of things "W.G." was nearing the end of his career, and in view of his unique service to the county, his outstanding position in the world of cricket, and especially of his known peculiarity of temperament, the imperious action of the Committee should not have been taken. What it must have cost the "Old Man" to sever his connection with his county in this deplorable manner, no one can tell, but it is certain that his anger quickly cooled off and he was never heard to speak an unkind word about his former colleagues. Three years passed, and the Committee passed another resolution:—

"That in recognition of his services to the Gloucestershire County Cricket Club, Dr. W. G. Grace be elected a life member of the Club."

That year, too, there was further evidence that the breach had been bridged over; the Gloucestershire team went up to the Crystal Palace and played the London County XI. I had the pleasure of accompanying them, and while walking across the ground before the game started the dear old man caught sight of me and came hurrying across with outstretched hand to welcome me, then catching hold of my arm lugged me away on a tour of inspection, for he was very proud of his ground, especially the bowling green. He was unfeignedly delighted to have his old team as guests, and those who played will not soon forget the lavish hospitality bestowed under his direction. The game was a remarkable one; Gloucestershire batted first and both the opening bats, T. H. Fowler and Wrathall, scored centuries, but "W.G." took 6 wickets in the first innings and then made 150. After being nearly 100 on, Gloucestershire collapsed, and lost by seven wickets; the Old Man must have been highly pleased at the result. In the return game at Gloucester, London County again won, this time by five wickets, and we saw him once more in 1908, when he came down to Bristol to take part in John Spry's benefit. What a welcome he received, and what a disappointment it was when he was soon out, caught and bowled, an incident which gave rise to a lot of discussion, some maintaining that on such an occasion the right course would have been to have missed the catch. Those who took this view could not have been practical cricketers or they would have known that nothing is more difficult than to deliberately miss a catch. One shudders to think what such a stickler for the canons of the game would have said had Thompson, the bowler, in this way broken the spirit of the game. Anyhow it is said that "W.G." heard of this discussion and gave his view very emphatically that the fielder played the game and no one had a right to criticise him.

CHAPTER XVII

Although " W.G." had left Gloucestershire, he continued
.o take part in important cricket for some years, and when the
Australians were over here in 1899 he played an admirable
innings against them for the South of England at the Crystal
Palace. It was at Nottingham during this season that the
Champion made his final appearance in a Test match. In
these days when so much store is set on youth and a man is
considered, in most branches of sport, a sort of Methuselah
at 40, it is hard to imagine a Test match player of 51, yet the
" Old Man " opened the innings and seemed well set for a big
score when he was out at 28 in trying to force the pace.

At Lord's, where he always seemed to be at home, he played
a fine innings of 50 for the M.C.C. and it is recorded that no
other English batsman was more at home with Ernest Jones,
the fastest and most dangerous bowler we have had on English
playing fields since Jack Crossland's time. In 1891-2 Jones
had bruised the Doctor all over the body in the opening game
of the tour, against Lord Sheffield's team, while in the Test
match at Lord's in 1896, the first ball this tear-away bowler
sent down, pitched deliberately very short, bounced and passed
through " W.G.'s " beard before going to the boundary for
four byes, but all the Champion said about it on the testimony
of the late Lord Harris was, " Whatever are ye at, Jones?"
In his fifty-first year, however, Dr. Grace was entirely at home
with all the Australian bowling that fine team of 1899 brought
to bear upon him until he had passed his half-century.

" W.G." continued to play in various representative games,
and in London County matches, until 1908, when his name
appeared for the last time in the first-class averages. In the
remaining years of his wonderful life he devoted himself to
club cricket, golf and bowls, and became as well-known in
the district in which he lived—Eltham, in Kent—as he was
around Bristol in the days of his youth, and he played for the
Eltham Club on July 26th, 1914, when he was 66 years of
age. His final appearance on the cricket field was at Catford

Bridge on Whit Monday, 1915, when he was the outstanding personality in a charity match.

The late Mr. F. S. Ashley-Cooper, whose knowledge of cricketers was unrivalled, has placed on permanent record a mass of statistical detail concerning Dr. Grace's cricket career and has shown that " W.G." played 568 completed innings for Gloucestershire, scoring 23,083 runs, and that his average was 40.56. Such an average would be outstanding for a few seasons, but it covers a period of 31 years. His highest average for the county was 80.90 for 11 innings in 1876; his lowest 19.78 in 1894. " W.G.'s " total number of wickets for Gloucestershire was 1,363 and the cost 18.36 each; from 1870 to 1889, he was one of the most effective bowlers in England and was never far behind the most successful bowlers who had no pretentions to skill as batsmen. There have been many all-rounders, but no other player has retained his form in both departments of the game over so long a period. Altogether " W.G." scored 126 centuries, full details of which will be found in the Appendix, and 53 of them were obtained for his county, 19 for the M.C.C., 15 for the Gentlemen v. the Players, 10 for South v. North, 7 for the Gentlemen of the South, 7 for London County, 6 for various other first-class teams, 4 for England, and 5 for the Gentlemen of England. Three times during his career he obtained two separate hundreds in one match, and he obtained three separate hundreds in successive matches, while he carried his bat through an innings on 17 occasions—a record which will probably stand for all time.

Apart from cricket, " W.G." was greatly interested and no mean performer in various other sports, in fact the only generally popular game which failed to appeal to him was lawn tennis. Whether he ever tried his hand at it is uncertain; there is no record of his having done so, but it is known that he was strongly opposed to the proposal to play an open tournament on the County Ground. Curiously enough, bowls, which offered such a contrast to cricket, was in great favour with the " Old Man," and although it is not generally known he took a foremost part in establishing international contests and for six years captained the English teams. Dr. Grace was also a most keen and enthusiastic golfer, and had the reputation of never missing a holeable putt, but it was not until after he had left Bristol that he devoted himself to this game, which was for him an ideal sport to satisfy his love for the open air, and the good companionship of kindred spirits.

Next to cricket, however, the sport which appealed to him most was beagling and this hard wearing exercise had a good deal to do with his amazing fitness, for he rarely missed an opportunity of being out with the Clifton Beagles, and though handicapped by his great weight was always one of the closest followers of hounds, no matter how hard the going. It is not easy to understand how Dr. Grace found time to satisfy his great love of sport, for in addition to those recreations already mentioned he was a very fine game shot, and with his friend, the late Mr. Herbert Gibbs, missed few opportunities that came his way of a day's shooting; and Mr. Gibbs' carefully kept game records indicate clearly that the Doctor's eye was as keen and steady in his quest for fur or feather as in compiling a century on a difficult wicket.

CHAPTER XVIII

We have now reached the last chapter in the history of the Grace brothers, who lived during a period which produced many famous Englishmen, some whose names will survive only for a time and then be known mainly to students of history, but the name and fame of Dr. W. G. Grace will live on as long as the British race retains a love of manly sport, and that surely will be for all time. " W.G." will become as much a figure of romance and inspiration as Sir Francis Drake, the great Elizabethan, or Lord Nelson in a later time; his mighty frame and big black beard will became a legend, and his incomparable deeds will be passed on as a tradition dear to every Britisher. It is strange to think that none of these big, strong, clean-living sons of Dr. Henry Mills Grace became old men as age is reckoned in these days. Those who saw " W.G." in the autumn of that year of national trial—1914—say that he was not greatly changed in aspect, and in spirit he was just the same old " W.G." as of yore, but the sands of his strenuous life were running out. Twice in 1914 he took his place among those with whom he had been associated in the game he loved; he was the central figure in the Centenary of Lord's Cricket Ground in June, while in August he attended Jack Hobbs' benefit match which was played on the same ground owing to the Oval having been taken over by the military authorities. He was not seen again in public, however, for the Great War had come; the German legions were smashing their way through Belgium, and although the call had come to the young men of Britain, cricketers were still hitting the loose ball to the boundary. Strange, isn't it, when the horrors of that awful period of 1914 are remembered that the peril of England was so little realised that county cricket went on as usual right through that fateful August and during the first week of September, and while our glorious little army of " old contemptibles " was fighting its way back from Mons and dying by thousands, first-class cricketers at home were still fighting for championship points. And not a voice was raised in protest, not a step was taken to stop the game until Dr.

W. G. Grace Gates at Lord's Cricket Ground.

W. G. Grace issued his clarion call to the cricketers of England; whatever others thought about the German menace, " W.G." had no doubts; and here is what he wrote in a letter to " The Sportsman ":—

> " There are many cricketers already doing their duty, but there are many more who do not seem to realise that in all probability they will have to serve either at home or abroad before the war is brought to a conclusion. The fighting on the Continent is very severe, and will probably be prolonged. I think the time has arrived when the County Cricket Season should be closed, for it is not fitting at a time like the present that able-bodied men should play day after day, and pleasure seekers look on. There are so many who are young and able, and are still hanging back. I should like to see all first-class cricketers of suitable age set a good example, and come to the help of their country without delay in its hour of need."

This was one of the very few occasions when a letter bearing his familiar name appeared in the public press, and it was worthy of his fame as a great Englishman. This letter was published on August 27th, but, like Drake of old, first-class cricketers decided to finish their games before making ready to get to grips with the enemy.

In the following year " W.G.'s " health began to give way, and while the young men of Kitchener's Army were pouring into France the announcement was made that he was seriously ill, followed by the sad news in October that he had passed away, and that it was thought that the noise and turmoil of a Zeppelin raid had hastened his end. The iron constitution, the exceptional physical fitness which he had preserved by a great love for the open-air life, failed him in his hour of need, and when he died on October 23rd, 1915, it was very hard to realise that this great man, who was remembered as the embodiment of strength and virility and astounding powers of endurance, was no more. But it was so,. and all over the British Empire the news was received with surprise and regret; even in Germany, the newspapers made a feature of his death, announcing that he had been the victim of an air-raid.

The funeral took place on October 26th at Elmer's End Cemetery, where his eldest son and daughter were buried, and despite the precarious times and the fact that so many were

serving their country in one way and another, there was a great
and representative gathering of relatives and friends to pay
final tribute to the King of Cricket. It is recorded that the last
scene was strikingly impressive and that many of those who
had been associated with Dr. Grace found it hard to repress
their grief as all that remained of this mighty man of cricket
passed to Mother Earth beneath the spreading branches of a
hawthorn tree.

There is much to be learnt by a study of " W.G.'s " cricket
career; much that would be of great benefit to the game for
which the champion did so much, for no one can point to an
occasion when he failed to consider the interests of his side
before his own personal gain in aggregate or average. All
through his life he held to the principle that it was the batsman's business to get runs and not to let the ball pass if it was
within striking distance, and he played his normal game under
all circumstances, memory providing no instance of the
Champion playing with the exaggerated caution, on a good
and true wicket, that is so common an experience for spectators when some of the most famous players of to-day are
batting. All the great bowlers of the past have confessed that
" W.G." made them feel that he was their master; even Alfred
Shaw, who had the Doctor's wicket more than any other
bowler, has acknowledged it. There are few batsmen to-day
who inspire such feelings until they are well set and feel safe.

Many have probably wondered what would have been the
view of " W.G." had he been living when the Australians
raised their protest against the tactics employed by D. R.
Jardine, the English Captain, to gain an advantage in the Tests
of 1932/33. My belief is that the " Old Man " would have
agreed with neither side; he would have held the Australians
in contempt for squealing, and would have been shocked by
the introduction of intensive fast bowling on the leg side as a
menace to the welfare of the game by making it a battle of
wits instead of skill.

It is passing strange that serious thought has not yet been
given to a memorial in Bristol to Dr. W. G. Grace. His
native village of Downend has set the great city in which he
lived and worked a notable example in this respect for they
have a fine playing field and pavilion which will always be
associated with the famous player who was born close by.

There is, however, nothing whatever in Bristol to associate one of the best known Englishmen with the city, not even a tablet on either of the houses in which he resided.

In 1948, the year which saw the 100th anniversary of " W.G.'s " birth, the Gloucestershire C.C.C. unanimously decided that in honour of this historic occasion the county ground at Bristol should be renamed " GRACE'S GROUND " and that a plaque should be placed at the main entrance in memory of the county's greatest cricketer. It was also agreed that the match against Derbyshire at Bristol on July 14th, 15th and 16th should be regarded as the Centenary match.

The 1948 Gentlemen v. Players match at Lord's was also regarded as the Centenary match .

CHAPTER XIX

No work dealing with the Grace family would be complete without a selection of those fascinating stories, both fact and fiction, which have arisen from the doings of the " brotherhood." Here are a few " Grace Stories," which are, perhaps, not so generally known. There has been much discussion as to whether " W.G." and his brothers, " E.M." and " G.F.," indulged in the habit of smoking, but the testimony of " young " Dr. E. M. Grace, son of the Coroner, who played so much for Thornbury and the Gloucestershire Gypsies, settles this query once and for all. He writes:—

> " None of the brothers smoked except Alfred. My father always said so and added that Alfred smoked enough for them all. Yet he lived the longest. My father only smoked once in his life, and that was a cigar, which made him so ill that he never smoked again."

W. A. Woof also substantiates this statement when he says that he played with the brothers from 1878, and at banquets at Canterbury, Cheltenham and elsewhere he never saw them smoke a pipe, cigar or cigarette, in fact in a match at Lord's between Smokers and Non-smokers, " W.G." played for the latter.

" W.G.," as is well known, was very fond of a practical joke, and one of his best bits of " kidding " was when Yorkshire were playing against Gloucestershire at Gloucester. Harrison, the fast bowler, was playing for the visitors and at the end of the match " W.G." told Woof that he was going to give Harrison half-a-sovereign if he could bowl W. A. Troup out in an hour, and that Woof was to tell him it would be easy. Poor Harrison bowled his fastest to Troup for half-an-hour, but failed to hit the wickets, and at the finish " W.G." thanked him and said, " That was the best bit of practice Troup has ever had; we are playing Lancashire tomorrow and it will do him a lot of good when he meets Jack Crossland." The expression on Harrison's face was a treat to watch, but " W.G." paid him for the practice.

Neither " W.G." nor " E.M." would permit barracking and in 1892 " E.M." was concerned in an incident which makes a very amusing story. The match was against Somerset on the County Ground, Bristol, and as " W.G." was standing down owing to leg trouble, " E.M." captained the team, and going in first with R. W. Rice, saw more than 100 put on before the first wicket fell. The wicket was a bit fiery, and Sam Woods, then at his best, was making the ball bump very awkwardly, but " E.M." stood up to him bravely, every now and then getting one on the knee or body which made him caper about. Some inconsiderate members of the crowd thought it good fun and began to shout at the veteran; for a while " E.M." took no notice, until a stinger from Sam hit him on the hand; " E.M." dropped his bat and began to rub his injured fingers. " Hold an inquest on't, Doctor!" shouted a man in the crowd. This was too much for the peppery veteran, and turning to H. T. Hewett the Somerset captain, he said, " Can I go after him?" Hewett assented, and off went the " little Doctor " in the direction from whence the remark had come—this was on the Orphan House side where the spectators were rather sparse. The spectators roared with delight, but the barracker didn't like the look of " E.M." and turning tail, ran towards the Ashley Hill gate, but the doctor did not give up the chase until the man had passed out of the ground. Returning to the pitch out of breath, amid a salvo of cheers, he picked up his bat and went on to score 70. What would have happened to the man, had he stood his ground, is open to conjecture, but I strongly suspect that " E.M." would have ordered him to leave the ground and finally tried to eject him.

" W.G.'s " faith in his own simple looking bowling and the fine fielding of Gilbert Jessop is shown in the following simple story. One of the last matches in which " W.G." played on the County Ground, Bristol, was against Hampshire. Mead was batting at the football end, and " W.G.," who was bowling, tossed up a simple looking one which the left-hander opened his shoulders to drive. It looked a certain boundary, but the batsman had reckoned without Jessop who was fielding at deep mid-off. Mead started to run, but before he reached the bowler's end, the middle stump was out of the ground, and the ball was travelling to the boundary at express speed. Jessop had caught the ball and making one of his lightning returns had also run Mead out.

One hot day " W.G." who was out walking with a friend in the country decided to knock at the door of a nearby cottage and ask for a glass of water. On doing so, a window above was opened and down came a bucket of dirty water, drenching both the Doctor and his companion. " W.G." was furious, but it was not until they reached a small hotel where they were able to borrow some dry garments, that they discovered the reason of their " wet welcome." A writ had been served on the old lady in the cottage, and she had taken " W.G." and his friend for a couple of bailiffs come to take possession.

It has already been related how " W.G." would only drink champagne on special occasions, but here is how one of his friends got round his objection. E. W. Ball, together with " W.G." and Sir Timothy O'Brien, had arranged to meet at the Imperial Hotel, Clifton, on the way to a match at Clifton College. Ted Ball suggested a bottle of champagne, but " W.G." refused saying that he never drank it except on special occasions. Ted Ball, however, disappeared and returned a few minutes later with a bottle under each arm. " I won't have it! " roared " W.G.," " I won't have it! Didn't I tell you I only took champagne on special occasions? " " This is a special occasion," replied Ball, " it's the anniversary of the Battle of Bannockburn. I've just looked it up!"

" W.G." has been reported to have been a somewhat indifferent after-dinner speaker, but here is a speech which proved that this is not exactly true. It was made by him acknowledging the testimonial presented to him in 1879. After thanking all his kind friends, " W.G." continued:—

> " And now, as you have said, my lord, I shall quit the cricket field for the surgery, though I still hope to spend the rest of my life in continual ' practice.' My time spent on cricket will not have been wasted. As a surgeon I shall often be called on to make a good ' cut ' at the end of a 'long drive,' whilst my experience in drawing stumps will encourage me to attempt dental surgery in all its branches. I have learned too to have patience both at the wicket and in the field. I only hope that patients will be forthcoming now. True it is that I have bowled many a maiden over in my time; but now to make up for that I hope to set many an one, ay, and many a matron too, on her legs again. My kind friends the cricket reporters have in writing of me at the wicket, often remarked that

I was well set. In future, my lord, I trust medical critics will say the same of my patients' broken legs and arms! And now I have done for I have never been in favour of ' a long stop.' "

Here is a story which indicates that " E.M." had a wonderful memory. It relates to a match at Thornbury, when Mr. Hamilton Ross, who played for Somerset in the 80's, hit " W.G." for five 6's in one over (there were five balls to an over in those days). The same year, when playing for Somerset against Gloucestershire, A. H. Evans called out to " W.G.": " Here's Hammie Ross says he hit you for five 6's in one over!" " I don't remember it," grumbled " W.G." " Ah," chimed in " E.M.," " that was the time you made more in one over than the whole of your side made in the rest of the innings." " W.G.," however, had his revenge in this very match, for he bowled Ross for a " duck " in each innings!

Although we have already recounted the two occasions when " W.G." helped to put back C. J. M. Fox's dislocated shoulder, there is still another occasion when his medical skill was of the greatest assistance on the cricket field—this time actually saving a fellow-cricketer's life. The match was Gloucestershire against Lancashire at Manchester in 1887 and the late A. C. M. Croome, who was fielding in the boundary, had the misfortune to fall against the railings, the sharp point of one entering his neck. The Doctor, however, was able to press the wound together and by holding it thus until further assistance arrived he undoubtedly saved the old Oxonian's life.

LIST OF CENTURIES

scored by W. G. Grace in first-class cricket

1866 (2)	224 not out.	England v. Surrey, at the Oval.
	173 not out.	Gentlemen of the South v. Players of the South, at the Oval.
1868 (3)	134 not out.	Gentlemen v. Players, at Lord's.
	130	South v. North of the Thames, at the Oval.
	102 not out.	South v. North of the Thames, at the Oval.
1869 (6)	180	Gentlemen v. Players of the South, at the Oval.
	138 not out.	M.C.C. v. Surrey, at Lords.
	127	M.C.C. v. Kent, at Lord's.
	122	South v. North, at the Oval.
	121	M.C.C. v. Notts, at Lord's.
	117	M.C.C. v. Oxford University, at Lord's.
1870 (5)	215	Gentlemen v. Players, at the Oval.
	172	Gloucestershire v. M.C.C., at Lord's.
	143	Gloucestershire v. Surrey, at the Oval.
	117 not out.	M.C.C. v. Notts, at Lord's.
	109	Gentlemen v. Players, at Lord's.
1871 (10)	268	South v. North, at the Oval.
	217	Gentlemen v. Players, at Brighton.
	189 not out.	Single v. Married of England, at Lord's.
	181	M.C.C. v. Surrey, at the Oval.
	178	South v. North, at the Oval.
	162	Gentlemen of England v. Cambridge University, at Cambridge.
	146	M.C.C. v. Surrey, at Lord's.

	118	Gentlemen of the South v. Gentlemen of the North, at West Brompton.
	117	M.C.C. v. Kent, at Lord's.
	116	Gloucester v. Notts, at Trent Bridge.
1872 (6)	170 not out.	England v. Notts and Yorks, at the Oval.
	150	Gloucestershire v. Yorkshire, at Sheffield.
	117	Gentlemen v. Players, at the Oval.
	114	South v. North, at the Oval.
	112	Gentlemen v. Players, at Lord's.
	101	M.C.C. v. Yorkshire, at Lord's.
1873 (7)	192 not out.	South v. North, at the Oval.
	163	Gentlemen v. Players, at Lord's.
	160 not out.	Gloucestershire v. Surrey, at Clifton.
	158	Gentlemen v. Players, at the Oval.
	152	XI v. XV of M.C.C., at Lord's.
	145	Gentlemen of the South v. Players of the North, at Prince's.
	134	Gentlemen v. Players of the South, at the Oval.
1874 (8)	179	Gloucestershire v. Sussex, at Brighton.
	167	Gloucestershire v. Yorkshire, at Sheffield.
	150	Gentlemen v. Players of the South, Oval.
	127	Gloucestershire v. Yorkshire, at Clifton.
	123	M.C.C. v. Kent, at Canterbury.
	121	Gloucester and Kent v. England, at Canterbury.
	110	Gentlemen v. Players, at Prince's.
	104	Gentlemen of South v. Players of the North, at Prince's.
1875 (3)	152	Gentlemen v. Players, at Lord's.
	119	Gloucestershire v. Notts, at Clifton.

	111		Gloucestershire v. Yorkshire, at Sheffield.
1876 (7)	344		M.C.C. v. Kent, at Canterbury.
	318	not-out.	Gloucestershire v. Yorkshire, at Cheltenham.
	177		Gloucestershire v. Notts, at Clifton.
	169		Gentlemen v. Players, at Lord's.
	126		United South v. United North, at Hull.
	114	not out.	South v. North, at Nottingham.
	104		Gloucestershire v. Sussex, at Brighton
1877 (2)	261		South v. North, at Prince's.
	110		Gloucester and Yorkshire v. England, at Lord's.
1878 (1)	116		Gloucestershire v. Notts, at Nottingham.
1879 (3)	123		Gloucestershire v. Surrey, at the Oval.
	113		Gloucestershire v. Somerset, at Clifton.
	102		Gloucestershire v. Notts, at Trent Bridge.
1880 (2)	152		England v. Australia, at the Oval.
	106		Gloucestershire v. Lancashire, at Clifton.
1881 (2)	182		Gloucestershire v. Notts, at Trent Bridge.
	100		Gentlemen v. Players, at the Oval.
1883 (1)	112		Gloucestershire v. Lancashire, at Clifton.
1884 (3)	116	not out.	Gloucester v. the Australians, at Clifton.
	107		Gent'emen of England v. the Australians, at the Oval.
	101		M.C.C. v. the Australians, at Lord's.
1885 (4)	221	not out.	Gloucestershire v. Middlesex, at Clifton.
	174		Gentlemen v. Players, at Scarborough.
	132		Gloucestershire v. Yorkshire, at Bradford.

	104	Gloucestershire v. Surrey, at Cheltenham.
1886 (4)	170	England v. Australia, at the Oval.
	148	Gentlemen of England v. the Australians, at the Oval.
	110	Gloucestershire v. the Australians, at Clifton.
	104	M.C.C. v. Oxford University, at Oxford.
1887 (6)	183 not out.	Gloucestershire v. Yorkshire, at Gloucester.
	116 not out.	M.C.C. v. Cambridge University, at Lord's.
	113 not out.	Gloucestershire v. Notts, at Clifton.
	113	Gloucestershire v. Middlesex, at Lord's.
	103 not out.	Gloucestershire v. Kent, at Clifton.
	101	Gloucestershire v. Kent, at Clifton.
1888 (4)	215	Gloucestershire v. Sussex, at Brighton.
	165	Gentlemen of England v. Australia, at Lord's.
	148	Gloucestershire v. Yorkshire, at Clifton.
	153	Gloucestershire v. Yorkshire, at Clifton.
1889 (3)	154	South v. North, at Scarborough.
	127 not out.	Gloucestershire v. Middlesex, at Cheltenham.
	101	Gloucestershire v. Middlesex, at Lord's.
1890 (1)	109	Gloucestershire v. Kent, at Maidstone.
1891-2 (1) in Australia.	159	Lord Sheffield's Team v. Victoria, at Melbourne.
1893 (1)	128	M.C.C. v. Kent, at Lord's.
1894 (3)	196	M.C.C. v. Cambridge University, at Lord's.
	139	M.C.C. v. Cambridge University, at Cambridge.

	131	Gentlemen v. Players, at Hastings.
1895 (9)	288	Gloucestershire v. Somerset, at Bristol.
	257	Gloucestershire v. Kent, at Gravesend.
	169	Gloucestershire v. Middlesex, at Lord's.
	125	M.C.C. v. Kent, at Lord's.
	118	Gentlemen v. Players, at Lord's.
	119	Gloucestershire v. Notts, at Cheltenham
	104	South v. North, at Hastings.
	103	M.C.C. v. Sussex, at Lord's.
	101 not out.	Gentlemen of England v. I. Zingari, at Lord's.

His 288 v. Somerset, at Bristol, was the Champion's 100th century.

1896 (4)	301	Gloucestershire v. Sussex, at Bristol.
	243 not out.	Gloucestershire v. Sussex, at Brighton.
	186	Gloucestershire v. Somerset, at Taunton.
	102 not out.	Gloucestershire v. Lancashire, at Bristol.
1897 (4)	131	Gloucestershire v. Notts, at Cheltenham.
	126	Gloucestershire v. Notts, at Nottingham.
	116	Gloucestershire v. Sussex, at Bristol.
	113	Gloucestershire v. the Philadelphians, at Bristol.
1898 (3)	168	Gloucestershire v. Notts, at Nottingham.
	126	Gloucestershire v. Essex, at Leyton.
	109	Gloucestershire v. Somerset, at Taunton.
1900 (3)	126	South v. North, at Lord's.
	110 not out.	London County Club v. Worcester.
	110	London County Club v. M.C.C. and Ground.
1901 (1)	132	London County Club, v. M.C.C. and Ground,

1902 (2)	131 not out.	London County v. M.C.C. and Ground.
	129	London County v. Warwickshire.
1903 (1)	150	London County v. Gloucestershire.
1904 (1)	166	London County v. M.C.C. and Ground.

All the last seven centuries were scored at the Crystal Palace.